Preventing
EARLY LEARNING
Failure

Edited by
Bob Sornson

ASCD

Association for Supervision and Curriculum Development
Alexandria, Virginia USA

®

Association for Supervision and Curriculum Development
1703 N. Beauregard St. • Alexandria, VA 22311-1714 USA
Telephone: 1-800-933-2723 or 703-578-9600 • Fax: 703-575-5400
Web site: http://www.ascd.org • E-mail: member@ascd.org

Printed in the United States of America.

ASCD Product No. 101003   s5/2001
ASCD member price: $19.95 nonmember price: $23.95

Library of Congress Cataloging-in-Publication Data
Preventing early learning failure / edited by Bob Sornson.
    p. cm.
Includes bibliographical references and index.
    ISBN 0-87120-510-6 (alk. paper)
    1. Early childhood education. 2. Learning. 3. Readiness for school.
I. Sornson, Robert. II. Association for Supervision and Curriculum Development.
    LB1139.23 .P74 2001
    372.21—dc21
                                         2001001200

---

07 06 05 04 03 02 01   10 9 8 7 6 5 4 3 2 1

PREVENTING EARLY LEARNING FAILURE

INTRODUCTION

Each year thousands of young children who have the capacity to experience school success and a love of learning do not. Some come to school without good early learning experiences and are unprepared for school learning activities. Others have experienced physical or emotional setbacks that cause them to be at risk of early learning failure.

Some children have never experienced parents who provide firm limits in a loving way, and they are not prepared to accept adults as authority figures. Others have had thousands of hours of access to entertainment systems that do not help develop attention, initiative, motor skills, social skills, or language.

Some children have mild deficits in auditory processing, visual processing, or motor skill development. Some children just develop a little more slowly than others and may need nothing more than additional time at the appropriate instructional tasks.

Most of these children have the potential to succeed in school and to become happy and productive learners. But often in our rush to cover important areas of instruction, we leave these children behind. They are not yet eligible for specialized teaching services or programs because they are not yet far enough behind.

In *Preventing Early Learning Failure*, the authors ask some basic questions that most schools have not yet fully addressed. Should we require several years of failure before support services are given to young learners? Are there proven and promising strategies that reduce the number of children who experience early learning failure? If we make a commitment to helping every possible child succeed in the early grades, will we have to rethink the way educators work with parents?

In Chapter 1, I open with a definition of the issue and point out practices in parenting, education, medicine, and the use of media that may contribute to early learning failure.

Chapters 2–8 describe practices that can help children find success in schools today. Richard Allington and Joyce McLeod look at what's most important in reading and math. Gary Hessler takes a careful look at the nature of true learning disabilities and how to distinguish fact from fantasy when it comes to deciding who is a disabled learner. Carol Flexer describes her research on the use of soundfield FM amplification in early elementary classrooms. Jim Tucker describes problem solving using the Instructional Support Team model, and Ken Pawlowski reports on an elementary school that has adopted that model and changed the lives of many at-risk learners. Nancy Sornson reports on a school that looks at basic sensory skill development at the kindergarten level. Ed Gickling and Verlinda Thompson reflect on the concepts and practices they have seen that make a difference in the lives of young learners.

Chapters 9–15 examine promising programs that every early childhood and elementary educator should know about. Bob Slavin describes the widely heralded Success for All program and Mildred Winter the Parents as Teachers program, designed to help families get children ready for early learning success. High/Scope's Larry Schweinhart describes preschool programs and principles that make a difference. Steve Kay and Craig Wheaton founded the 1,000 Days to Success program and offer no excuses if a child fails to learn. Peter Kline looks at teaching and learning that use an awareness of multiple intelligences and individual learning needs. Tom Johnson describes Project First Step, a program that lets classroom teachers encourage the development of needed motor skills.

Chapters 16–18 include stories that allow the reader to imagine some of the ways to implement prevention practices. Jim Fay tells a story about a classroom teacher who learned to think differently about behavior. Kaye Mentley and Sally Ludwig describe three children at the Huntington Woods School, and I relate a story about the benefits that can result from true cooperation between parent and teacher.

In the final chapter, I ask readers to join me in considering the hopes and challenges of educators who commit themselves to the success of every child.

Please share this book with every teacher, administrator, legislator, school board member, and community leader who believes with you that we cannot afford to let children in the early years of school fall into a pattern of failure that will affect the children, their families, and their communities throughout a lifetime.

BOB SORNSON
2001

MANUFACTURING EARLY LEARNING FAILURE

Bob Sornson

Sam, a bright-eyed 4-year-old boy, is being raised to become learning disabled. His family is intact. His parents love him. There is no abuse in the home. He did not experience prenatal exposure to drugs. Yet, he is doing poorly in preschool and moving quickly toward experiencing early learning failure.

Some of the other moms at preschool urged Sam's mom to seek help. Good for them! So many of us are afraid to interfere in the lives of our neighbors. And good for Sam's mom for being willing to look for answers! She knows she has a problem.

Sam is a beautiful boy. At least his nose looked beautiful as he sat with his jacket pulled up around his head in my office. "Are you nervous, sweetheart?" said his mom with concern. He disappeared under his coat. After a moment the eyes reappeared. They shone. "Would you like to sit on Mommy's lap?" Again, the head disappeared.

After I learned that Sam's mom was concerned about his inability to stay focused on a task and his unpredictable behaviors, she left us so that I might have a chance to see who was hiding under the coat. We played catch and balanced. We tried to skip and hop. We played memory games and drew pictures. We talked. Then it was time for Sam to go to the waiting room and his mom to work with me.

Well-educated and smart, Sam's mom was eager for ideas. First, we discussed what is working well. Sam is a great talker once he emerges from his coat. He has lots of ideas and good auditory memory. He holds a pencil nicely, can draw adequately, and throws a ball hard. However, there are deficits. His behaviors at school and home are the most obvious concerns, but other problems contribute to a pattern. He watches way too much television, and his balance is underdeveloped as is his general coordination. He can't skip or use the two sides of his body well together. He has difficulty crossing midline and exhibits poor fine-motor and visual-motor skills. He can't catch because his depth-perception skills are underdeveloped. His articulation of some sounds is poor.

As we talked, Sam's mom filled in the missing pieces. Sam has had a long history of ear infections and heavy antibiotic use until tubes were inserted. He continues to be chronically stuffy, and she thinks he's allergic to some foods, but the doctor wants to wait before trying to deal with any allergies. Sam doesn't really have any friends, and sometimes he's mean to his little brother. He loves television and videos, and they are buying him his own computer with lots of games for Christmas. He's enrolled in a Tae Kwon Do class, but mostly he fails to pay attention.

Sam has a limited diet. He refuses to eat most foods and often insists on eating in front of the television. The only foods he'll eat are cheese sandwiches, cheese, milk, ice cream, candy, and chicken nuggets. When asked to go to time-out at home or at school, he refuses.

Poor Sam. The raw ingredients for manufacturing unnecessary early learning failure are in place: poor control over Sam's behavior, especially time-out and food choices; a sedentary lifestyle; too much video; a poor diet; lots of ear infections; overuse of antibiotics; poor auditory discrimination and articulation; poor balance; poor gross-motor, fine-motor, and visual-motor skills; and poor depth perception. Somehow, with all this, Sam thinks he's running the show.

Learning at school won't be easy for Sam unless things change soon. Children like Sam don't like to do what the teacher says, don't make friends easily, aren't ready to sit still, don't engage in near-point visual activity such as cutting, drawing, or making letters, don't struggle to listen, and don't understand basic mathematical concepts.

The manufacturing of unnecessary early learning failure is at an all-time high. Children come to school less developmentally ready to learn than ever before. Ask kindergarten or 1st-grade teachers anywhere. More and more children with language delays, motor-skill delays, and outrageous behavior problems are coming to school. Some of them look up at their adult teachers and say, "I don't have to do what you say!", correctly reflecting the experience they've had with adults to date.

The manufacturing of early learning failure has many allies. The incredibly attractive variety of video entertainment options helps keep kids

2

sedentary, quiet, and out of our hair. Time better spent playing, talking, imagining, working with Mom or Dad, negotiating with neighborhood children, listening, cuddling, drawing, or enjoying nature is not available.

The lack of support networks for parents also is a factor. Who helps parents learn on the job? Although there are wonderful books and tapes on parenting, many parents learn this most important role on their own. Churches and schools offer little support. Neighbors usually mind their own business. Media and popular culture models of parenting leave a lot to be desired. Sam's parents have been trying to figure out parenting on their own.

The medical community is also helping manufacture early learning failure in its own way. Few doctors have the time to talk about parenting practices, or to instruct parents in how to look for mucus reactions to particular foods or environmental factors, on the importance of nutrition, on the need to set limits on television viewing, on the need for movement, or on how to encourage visual-motor play. The overuse of antibiotics may be related to some chronic developmental problems.

The future of our schools and our society demands that we move quickly to prevent early learning failure. Sam doesn't have to fail, nor do millions of other children who come to school at risk of learning failure. Early successful learning experiences lay the foundation for positive self-concept, love of learning, and a reduced likelihood of every dangerous adolescent behavior. Children who are poor readers in the early grades usually stay poor readers. The same is true for poor math skills and antisocial behavior.

Schools can reduce early learning failure by changing practices and programs. There are many successful initiatives around the country: Reading Recovery, Success for All, Prevention of Learning Disabilities, and Instructional Support Teams are proven approaches. Some schools have used small class size, multi-age classrooms, soundfield FM amplification, instruction based on multiple intelligences, or motor development programs to help children get ready to succeed. Some schools have reached out to parents like never before, believing that a learning community at school where parents feel valued and respected is necessary to help children succeed.

Churches can help by recognizing how isolated many parents are in today's culture and by establishing classes and mentoring relationships. The medical community can help by looking carefully at the whole child and seeing him as part of a family system.

In the fall, Sam will be eligible for kindergarten. There's a lot of work to be done before he's ready, and it can't all be done at once. Trying to prioritize, I'd probably put getting control of time-out and food choices at home on the top of my list. Then I'd cut television and get more activity into his life. Dealing with his chronic mucus drainage might come next—

with the help of a good doctor. Fifteen minutes a day of balance activities and ball play to develop depth perception would be incredibly helpful, followed by encouraging table games for the development of visual-motor skills. If his head is clear of mucus, his balance is developing, and his behaviors are reasonably under control, I'm sure that listening skills would develop from good conversations at home and school.

Sam has not experienced the ideal developmental pattern in the early years—a pattern that allows most learning to occur through play and that helps a child feel ready to meet new challenges. But it's not too late. With luck, Sam can do a little catching up, be ready for the primary grades, and never experience the debilitating effects of early learning failure.

TEACHING CHILDREN TO READ: WHAT REALLY MATTERS

Richard L. Allington

I n every nation, there are some children who find learning to read difficult regardless of the nature of the writing system, the assessment plan, the national wealth, or the organization of the educational system (Elley, 1992). Even when offered good instruction, some children struggle mightily to become literate. Unfortunately, too many children struggle because they do not have access to sufficient instruction. But just how can sufficient instruction be characterized? In other words, what is it that really matters in designing and delivering instruction to children who find learning to read difficult?

After a century of research on reading instruction and on children who find learning to read difficult, only a few things of critical instructional importance have been identified (Allington, 2001). Unfortunately, professional debates and discussions often ignore each of these important dimensions of effective instructional environments and interventions.

PROFESSIONAL BELIEFS MATTER

Since the study of reading difficulties began around the turn of the 20th century, three broad factors have been touted regularly as sources of reading difficulties: the intelligence factor, the "disadvantage" factor, and the

Adapted from Allington, R. L. (1998). Introduction. In R. L. Allington (Ed.), *Teaching struggling readers*. Newark, DE: International Reading Association. Copyright © 1998 by the International Reading Association.

learning disabilities factor. Each of these factors is based on the beliefs of educators and remains influential in school response to the problem of reading difficulties (Johnston & Allington, 1991).

THE INTELLIGENCE FACTOR

First, limited intellectual abilities were viewed as a primary source of the difficulties. But then it was discovered that achievement on purported measures of intelligence and measures of reading achievement did not actually correlate that well. In fact, terms were invented—hyperlexia and dyslexia—to explain aberrations for those children who read better or less well than expected. But when educators believed that intelligence, or the lack of it, was the source of difficulty, little was offered in the way of instructional interventions because some children were just never going to be readers due to limited intellectual capacity. Some children were just "slow learners" and not much could be expected of them. Thus, the "slow it down and make it concrete" instructional plan was widely implemented, virtually ensuring that some children developed only minimal levels of reading proficiency (Allington, 1991).

THE "DISADVANTAGE" FACTOR

However, after noting the less-than-perfect correlation between measures of intellect and measures of reading, other explanations emerged. Probably the most popular was targeting "disadvantage"—both economic and educational—as a source of the difficulties (McGill-Franzen, 1987). This explanation got a boost from research showing that many more poor children had difficulty learning to read. Thus, interventions were developed in the hopes of overcoming the disadvantages of poverty. But few of these programs actually seemed to enhance the instruction children received, and in some cases the older "slow it down" plan was continued with "disadvantaged" children (Allington, 1991; McGill-Franzen, 1994). Consequently, many of the "disadvantaged" children failed to develop into readers and writers even after participating in the compensatory education programs (Puma, Jones, Rock, & Fernandez, 1993). Some educators and researchers argued that schools just could not be expected to overcome the negative effects of growing up poor. But the "disadvantage" conceptualization shaped the sorts of instructional programs that were offered.

THE LEARNING DISABILITIES FACTOR

A third and more recently popularized belief about children who find learning to read difficult is that these children suffer a disability (McGill-Franzen, 1987). Usually this disability is characterized in terms of neurological damage or difference that makes perceptual or verbal learning exceedingly difficult, if not impossible. But evidence of a neurological basis for reading difficulties has been difficult to find. If children with such conditions exist, they exist in incredibly small numbers—far too few to account for the range of difficulties now observed (Vellutino et al., 1996). Nonetheless, believing in a neurologically based disability meant that some children could not be expected to learn to read, and so little effective instruction was offered (Allington & McGill-Franzen, 1989). For instance, few individualized educational plans set annual goals for accelerated literacy development (an annual goal of 1.5 years growth per year, for instance) because the disability conceptualization suggested damaged or limited capacity for learning.

CURRENT PROFESSIONAL BELIEFS

Most recently, there has been a growing recognition that reading acquisition is relatively easy for some children and relatively difficult—exceedingly difficult in a few cases—for other children. But it seems that only a few children cannot acquire reading proficiency alongside their peers (Lyons, Pinnell, & DeFord, 1993; Vellutino et al., 1996). This might be labeled the "sufficiency of instruction" conceptualization. Because children vary in the ease with which they acquire literacy and because they arrive at school with varied levels of literacy experience, we should expect that providing a standard instructional program would result in large discrepancies in achievement. Only when the instructional program offers varied levels of instructional intensity can we reasonably expect all children to develop reading proficiency—especially developing that proficiency on a schedule similar to peer development.

However, we must first believe that virtually all children can become readers before we even begin to think about how to design instruction to ensure that this happens (Winfield, 1986; Zigmond, 1993). This belief leads us to design programs in which some children have access to larger amounts of higher quality and more intensive instruction.

Beliefs are important because they drive our thinking, our planning, and our actions (Allington, McGill-Franzen, & Schick, 1997). Yet, for too long, our professional beliefs have resulted in educational efforts that produced some children who remained largely illiterate. Believing in the inherent educability of all children is a necessary first step in creating schools where all children become readers and writers. Creating such schools involves developing instructional environments that display the following characteristics (Allington, 2001):

Children need to read a lot to become good readers. In addition to professional beliefs, it also matters how successful we are at creating instructional environments that foster wide reading by all children, but especially by those children who have found learning to read difficult. Unfortunately, an overwhelmingly consistent finding in the research is that children who find learning to read difficult often participate in educational programs that fail to foster much reading at all—these children do less guided reading with their teachers and less independent, voluntary reading (Krashen, 1993).

Only occasionally are interventions purposefully designed to alter this situation (Morrow, 1992). More often the instruction for children who find learning to read difficult occupies them with skill games, practice dittos, and drills (Allington, 1983; Allington & McGill-Franzen, 1989). In some schools children who have difficulty with reading have no books in their desks that they can actually read or use to learn to read (Allington, 2001). These deficiencies occur even though schools spend substantial funds on interventions intended to assist the struggling readers (Guice, Allington, Johnston, Baker, & Michelson, 1996).

The instructional environment needs to be rich in reading resources. If children are going to engage in substantial amounts of reading, at least two aspects of the instructional environment must be attended to. First, children need access to a large supply of books of appropriate difficulty, books that fit the "Goldilocks principle" (Fountas & Pinnell, 1996), i.e., they are not too hard and not too easy, but just right. Children can read these books fluently while also understanding the story or information. This is not a new idea. For most of the past century, fitting children to books has been advocated, and teachers have been taught to administer informal reading inventories and, more recently, to gather running records in an attempt to ensure appropriate book placement. In some schools, unfortunately, there is little evidence that this feature of appropriate instruction is of much concern. For instance, we too often still find classrooms where all children are taught from the same book, regardless of how well the book matches their level of literacy development. We find remedial and special education programs that offer little support to either children or classroom teachers in this regard (McGill-Franzen, 1994). Many programs exert little effort to ensure that struggling readers have easy access to a large supply of appropriate books. We find state educational policies that support the purchase of more skill and drill workbooks and more test preparation materials, while classrooms have few, if any, books appropriate for the children having difficulty with reading acquisition, and school libraries remain underfunded, understaffed, and understocked.

If we want to foster wider reading, there is another feature of instructional environments that is important but often overlooked. Children need access to books and stories that are interesting and engaging to them, and they need the freedom to choose at least some of the books they read, especially if we are attempting to foster independent, voluntary reading. Again, however, too few efforts to help children who find learning to read difficult are focused on ensuring that a supply of interesting and appropriately difficult books is readily available.

Often we hear talk of the need to motivate reluctant readers, but perhaps we should think more about examining carefully the environments we create, rather than characterizing the lack of voluntary reading as a motivational problem located in children. We need to worry more about putting enticing, just-right books in children's hands and less about schemes that attempt to bribe children into taking home an uninteresting book that is too difficult.

Children need to be taught to read. Although there may be some natural readers, most children need good instruction, and some need enormous amounts of personalized instruction if they are to become readers. Research on effective instruction suggests that we have not yet found a way to package good teaching. In study after study, it is the quality of the teacher, not variation in curriculum materials, that is identified as the critical factor in effective instruction (Bond & Dykstra, 1997; Darling-Hammond, 1999; Knapp, 1995; Shanklin, 1990). That is not to say that materials are wholly unimportant, but that investing in teacher development has a better result than investing in curriculum materials. Good teachers—expert teachers—produce more readers than other teachers regardless of the curriculum materials used.

Good teachers know their students better and are more precise in targeting instructional needs (Johnston, 1997). Good teachers know more about literacy acquisition and use this expertise in planning instruction. They offer a more comprehensive sort of reading instruction, with more attention to individual instructional needs (Pressley et al., 1996). These teachers create literacy-rich classrooms and teach strategies using explicit modeling. In other words, these teachers do not just assign work or attempt to cover some segment of the curriculum material. Instead, they teach actively and teach the useful strategies students need when they need them, as opposed to following some predetermined schedule or pacing (Duffy, 1997). These teachers also push children to become more independent, more thoughtful readers.

Good teachers create classrooms where reading and writing activity fill large blocks of time. They develop effective decoding strategies, spelling strategies, and composing and comprehension activities, and they are constantly monitoring children's reading development and intervening when instruction is needed (Goatley, Brock, & Raphael, 1995).

But some children need more intensive instruction than a classroom teacher can provide. Some children will need additional small group work, and some can be expected to need tutorial assistance. Some children will need such help only for the short term, while others will need assistance for the long term. In other words, some children will need extra instruction this Wednesday after school, some will need a tutorial all next week, and some will need the added time that a summer school experience would provide for the remainder of their school career. Unfortunately, all too often we have designed extra-instructional programs in a one-size-fits-all scheme (Walmsley & Allington, 1995), in which everyone will receive three 30-minute small-group sessions every week all year, regardless of their real needs. Almost no one will participate in tutoring because educators have not devised a plan that makes short-term tutoring available, even though this is generally more successful than other efforts (Wasik & Slavin, 1993).

Until we redesign school programs so that children have access to sufficient instruction—of whatever level of intensity and duration is needed—then we will have children who will struggle with reading acquisition when compared with their peers. The key to success is good teachers working within a flexible school framework that allows them to provide the instruction children need.

Schools work better when families are partners. Good schools are more important to literacy development than are families (Snow, Barnes, Chandler, Goodman, & Hemphill, 1991), but the most successful schools have fostered and supported family involvement. It is schools, not families, that are charged with responsibility for developing reading proficiency. Inviting family involvement, providing families with support in working with their children, and gaining the confidence of the families of children attending the school are all wonderfully important tasks to be undertaken after the school has ensured the adequacy of the school program.

Creating schools where children are neither rewarded nor penalized for their socio-economic status must be the first task of educators (Allington

& Cunningham, 2001). Once effective school programs are in place—programs that provide children with access to sufficient high-quality instruction—then work on family support and involvement efforts can proceed. Interestingly, once good school programs are in place, family involvement often seems less of a problem.

Developing strategies to support families should be the first order of business. For instance, schools might work to ensure that all children have an adequate supply of appropriate books to take home in the evening or over the weekend. Extending this support further might involve opening the school library evenings, on weekends, and over the summer. In some schools this has been accomplished with no added costs by using flexible scheduling of library staff.

Many families simply do not have the discretionary funds to purchase books for a child's bedroom library. A recent California study reported home supplies of appropriate books varied widely by community, with the wealthiest homes reporting an average of nearly 200 age-appropriate books in each household and the least wealthy homes reporting one age-appropriate book available in every other household (Smith, Constantino, & Krashen, 1997). Often the local elementary school has the largest supply of children's books in the near vicinity and yet that supply often is largely unavailable to the parents of children who own no books of their own. To address this problem, schools might develop sponsorships for book giveaway programs so that every child receives a number of personal books each year. Schools also might invite parents of preschool-age children to use the library.

Families can support school learning in other ways, but many will need substantial guidance and support to help effectively. We need to understand that literacy experiences differ across families, and family ability to support school instruction also varies (Purcell-Gates, 1995). It often seems that schools would do better to make a greater effort to learn from families than to assume that families need to be taught or told what to do.

So What Do We Do First?

There are only a few things that really matter in developing avid and proficient readers. A good beginning is trying to evaluate reliably just how those things that really matter are addressed in your school:

• Do children who find learning to read difficult have easy access to appropriate and engaging books and stories?

• Has the instructional program been designed to offer children access to reading instruction of sufficient quality and intensity to accelerate their literacy development?

• Is the instruction exemplary and focused on developing independent, engaged readers?

• Are families provided support in helping their children become readers?

Although there are only a few things that really matter, creating schools that work well for all children is not easy. Changing schools is hard work. It takes time, energy, and expertise. Individuals hold the key in those matters. It is up to you.

REFERENCES

Allington, R. L. (1983). The reading instruction provided readers of differing abilities. *The Elementary School Journal, 83,* 548–559.

Allington, R. L. (1991). The legacy of "slow it down and make it more concrete." In J. Zutell & S. McCormick (Eds.), *Learner factors/teacher factors: Issues in literacy research and instruction* (pp. 19–30). Chicago: National Reading Conference.

Allington, R. L. (2001). *What really matters for struggling readers: Designing research-based programs.* New York: Longman.

Allington, R. L., & Cunningham, P. M. (2001). *Schools that work: Where all children read and write* (2nd ed.). New York: Longman.

Allington, R. L., & McGill-Franzen, A. (1989). Different programs, indifferent instruction. In A. Gartner & D. Lipsky (Eds.), *Beyond separate education: Quality education for all* (pp. 75–98). Baltimore: Brookes.

Allington, R. L., McGill-Franzen, A., & Schick, R. (1997). How administrators understand learning difficulties: A qualitative analysis. *Remedial and Special Education, 18*(4), 223–232.

Bond, G. L., & Dykstra, R. (1997, October–December). The cooperative research program in first grade reading instruction. *Reading Research Quarterly, 32*(4), 348–427.

Darling-Hammond, L. (1999). *Teacher quality and student achievement: A review of state policy evidence.* Seattle: Center for the Study of Teaching and Policy.

Duffy, G. G. (1997). Powerful models or powerful teachers? An argument for teacher-as-entrepreneur. In S. Stahl & D. Hayes (Eds.), *Instructional models in reading* (pp. 351–365). Hillsdale, NJ: Erlbaum.

Elley, W. B. (1992). *How in the world do students read? IEA study of reading literacy.* The Hague, Netherlands: International Association for the Evaluation of Educational Achievement.

Fountas, I. C., & Pinnell, G. S. (1996). *Guided reading: Good first teaching for all children.* Portsmouth, NH: Heinemann.

Goatley, V. J., Brock, C. H., & Raphael, T. E. (1995). Diverse learners participating in regular education "Book Clubs." *Reading Research Quarterly, 30,* 352–380.

Guice, S., Allington, R. L., Johnston, P., Baker, K., & Michelson, N. (1996, Summer). Access?: Books, children, and literature-based curriculum in schools. *The New Advocate, 9*(3), 197–207.

Johnston, P. A. (1997). *Knowing literacy.* York, ME: Stenhouse.

Johnston, P. A., & Allington, R. L. (1991). Remediation. In R. Barr, M. Kamil, P. Mosenthal, & P. D. Pearson (Eds.), *Handbook of reading research: Volume II* (pp. 984–1012). White Plains, NY: Longman.

Knapp, M. S. (1995). *Teaching for meaning in high-poverty classrooms.* New York: Teachers College Press.

Krashen, S. (1993). *The power of reading: Insights from the research.* Englewood, CO: Libraries Unlimited.

Lyons, C. A., Pinnell, G. S., & DeFord, D. E. (1993). *Partners in learning: Teachers and children in Reading Recovery.* New York: Teachers College Press.

McGill-Franzen, A. (1987). Failure to learn to read: Formulating a policy problem. *Reading Research Quarterly, 22,* 475–490.

McGill-Franzen, A. M. (1994). Is there accountability for learning and belief in children's potential? In E. H. Hiebert & B. M. Taylor (Eds.), *Getting reading right from the start: Effective early literacy interventions.* Boston: Allyn & Bacon.

Morrow, L. M. (1992). The impact of a literature-based program on literacy achievement, use of literature, and attitudes of children from minority backgrounds. *Reading Research Quarterly, 27,* 250–275.

Pressley, M., Wharton-McDonald, R., Ranking, J., Mistretta, J., Yokoi, L., & Ettenberger, S. (1996). The nature of outstanding primary grade literacy instruction. In E. McIntyre & M. Pressley (Eds.), *Balanced instruction: Strategies and skills in whole language* (pp. 251–276). Norwood, MA: Christopher-Gordon.

Puma, M. J., Jones, C. C., Rock, D., & Fernandez, R. (1993). *Prospects: The congressionally mandated study of educational growth and opportunity—The interim report* (GPO No. 19930-354–886 QL3). Washington, DC: U.S. Department of Education.

Purcell-Gates, V. (1995). *Other people's words: The cycle of low literacy.* Cambridge, MA: Harvard University Press.

Shanklin, N. L. (1990). Improving the comprehension of at-risk readers: An ethnographic study of four Chapter I teachers, grades 4–6. *International Journal of Reading, Writing, and Learning Disabilities, 6,* 137–148.

Smith, C., Constantino, R., & Krashen, S. (1997). Differences in print environment: Children in Beverly Hills, Compton and Watts. *Emergency Librarian, 24,* 8–9.

Snow, C., Barnes, W., Chandler, J., Goodman, I. F., & Hemphill, L. (1991). *Unfulfilled expectations: Home and school influences on literacy.* Cambridge, MA: Harvard University Press.

Vellutino, F. R., Sipay, E. R., Small, S. G., Pratt, A., Chen, R, & Denckla, M. B. (1996). Cognitive profiles of difficult-to-remediate and readily remediated poor readers: Early intervention as a vehicle for distinguishing between cognitive and experiential deficits as basic causes of specific reading disability. *Journal of Educational Psychology, 88,* 601–638.

Walmsley, S. A., & Allington, R. L. (1995). Redefining and reforming instructional support programs for at-risk students. In R. L. Allington & S. A. Walmsley (Eds.), *No quick fix: Rethinking literacy programs in America's elementary schools* (pp. 19–41). New York: Teachers College Press.

Wasik, B. A. & Slavin, R. E. (1993). Preventing early reading failure with one-on-one tutoring: A review of five programs. *Reading Research Quarterly, 28,* 178–200.

Winfield, L. F. (1986). Teachers' beliefs toward academically at-risk students in inner urban schools. *Urban Review, 18,* 253–268.

Zigmond, N. (1993). Learning disabilities from an educational perspective. In G. R. Lyon, D. B. Gray, J. F. Kavanagh, & N. A. Krasgegor (Eds.), *Better understanding learning disabilities: New views from research & their implications for education & public policies* (pp. 229–250). Baltimore: Brookes.

BUILDING EARLY NUMERACY SKILLS

Joyce McLeod

Young children come to preschool and kindergarten with a great deal of intuitive understanding and knowledge about numbers, as evidenced by these young learners' statements:

- "I'm 5 years old," while holding up five fingers.
- "I can count to 100!" as the child begins the singsong chant of "1, 2, 3..."
- "She has more pieces of candy than I do," spoken in an indignant tone.
- "He has a bigger piece than I do," as the child compares the size of two pieces of pizza or two halves of a sandwich.
- "I had it first!" as the child tugs at a toy another child has snatched. Ordinal position is very important to young children!
- "100 pieces of candy are a lot of pieces," as the child mentally compares quantities using benchmarks of more than and less than.
- "I have five pennies," as the child opens his or her hand and point counts to name the cardinal number of the group of pennies.

Then formal instruction in mathematics begins! Learning objectives are written; benchmarks for achieving standards are set; instruction aligned with standards is planned; and teachers are instructed to look ahead and prepare students for the high-stakes tests that are in the not-too-distant future. Teachers begin teaching the concepts, skills, and applications defined by the standards. And then, much to teachers' dismay, many children do not make smooth progress toward accomplishment of the standards, and many show significant gaps in their conceptual understanding and skill development.

DEFINING EARLY CHILDHOOD NUMERACY SKILLS

The National Council of Teachers of Mathematics *Principles and Standards for School Mathematics* (NCTM, 2000) define what children should know and be able to do and the range of grade levels at which the defined standards should be achieved. For example, this document establishes standards for prekindergarten through grade 2 as the first range of grade levels. It also defines the content and process standards of mathematics that many schools and districts across the United States will use to develop the formal mathematics curriculum for their students. The content standards are Number and Operations, Algebra, Geometry, Measurement, and Data Analysis and Probability. The process standards are problem solving, connections, reasoning and proof, communication, and representation.

The hierarchical and sequential nature of mathematics requires that children accomplish earlier standards within a content standard as a prerequisite to accomplishing higher-level standards. For example, in the Number and Operations strand, a major goal for the early years is that children reach the level of automaticity with the basic addition and subtraction facts. Automaticity is defined as the ability to give a sum or difference for a basic fact (usually defined as numbers with sums to 18 or differences of numbers subtracted from 18) in less than three seconds, without counting or using fingers or other external helps (Van de Walle, 1998).

The following sequence of development ensures that children can reach the point of automaticity with the addition facts:

• Comparison of groups of objects to identify the relationships of more than, less than, or the same number using visual skills rather than counting;
• Rote counting to list the counting words in order;
• Point counting, using one-to-one matching to count a group of objects, to identify the cardinal number of the group;
• Writing and recognizing numerals;
• Building number relationships, such as 5 is 1 more than 4 and 1 less than 6, and part-part-whole relationships, such as 6 may be thought of as a group of 2 and a group of 4 or two groups of 3;

• Naming the number of objects in patterned arrangements without counting, i.e., naming the number on dot cards in different arrangements of a number;

• Understanding the number 10 as a benchmark number since it is the basis of the decimal place-value system;

• Understanding the operation of addition as joining two groups to find how many in all;

• Developing efficient strategies that can be done mentally and quickly to help children retrieve facts as they strive toward memorization. Such strategies include one-more-than and two-more-than facts related to number relationships developed earlier; facts with zero as one addend, such as 6+0 = 6; doubles, which are facts in which both addends are the same, such as 6+6 = 12; near doubles, which are facts which include all combinations where one addend is one more than the other, such as 6+7 = (6+6)+1, or all combinations where one addend is 8 or 9 in which children build on to the 8 or 9 up to 10 and then add on, such as 8+5 = 8+2(or 10)+3 = 13; and

• Understanding and using the order property to reduce the number of facts to be memorized.

Therefore, automaticity with the addition facts requires much more than just rote memory. For these facts to become part of a child's long-term memory and, therefore, a conditioned response when given a fact, they must be linked together in related ways. As children work through this hierarchy of concepts and skills, connections between the mathematical ideas, connections to standards in other disciplines, and connections to everyday events will facilitate making the learning more permanent. Making number relationships relevant—such as counting sets of silverware as they set the table at home and adding to find how many pieces of paper are needed for two groups of children—helps children remember and recall what they have learned.

As we have learned more about how the brain learns, the importance of making the learning relevant so it links to prior knowledge and experience has been verified as a critical strategy (Jensen, 1998). Building networks of related concepts and skills facilitates building long-term memory. Making sure that children have mastered the earlier concepts and skills before moving to higher-level concepts and skills ensures that these networks are in place and will help the child make continuous progress, which is the only basis upon which successful achievement in mathematics can be built.

PREVENTING EARLY LEARNING FAILURE AND ITS LIFELONG CONSEQUENCES

How can we ensure that every child has the opportunity to make continuous progress in working along a continuum of concepts and skills to accomplish benchmark standards? The following strategies built into the beliefs and practices of educators will ensure that each child can experience early learning success:

• Instruction must begin at the appropriate point in the curriculum, or at an appropriate instructional level, based on a careful diagnosis of each child's present evidence of conceptual development, skill proficiency, and ability to apply mathematics to everyday situations. Instructional strategies should vary, should focus on a child's preferred learning styles and modalities, and should be related to the child's own experience. Teachers should use a scaffolding approach that involves modifying different levels of support, from the least amount of assistance to an increasing amount of assistance (Valencia & Wixson, 1991).

• Rote learning must follow a carefully sequenced set of experiences based on the standards for mathematics that guide children along a path of both conceptual understanding and skill proficiency.

• The focus of the classroom mathematics program should be to help children develop the understanding that mathematics is a network of related concepts and skills, not isolated skills to be learned only at the rote memory level.

• Manipulative activities must be structured so that interactions between teacher and children and among the children help them "see" the relationships of a model (either concrete or pictorial) to the abstract symbols that record the relationship. The use of manipulatives does not guarantee understanding—it is the child's prior knowledge and experience and the interaction with the manipulatives that guide understanding (Meira, 1998).

• If a child does not accomplish a given objective or benchmark, appropriate interventions must be done before moving ahead in the curriculum, so that the child does not enter a cycle of failure and futile attempts at remediation.

A child who has gaps in his or her mathematical achievement at the early levels is forever at a disadvantage in trying to catch up or keep up. It is simply impossible, for example, for a child to understand the concepts of multiplication and division, memorize the multiplication and division facts, and choose multiplication or division as the appropriate operation to solve a problem if he or she has not developed these concepts and skills for addition and subtraction and an understanding of the inverse relationships between these operations.

The sequential nature of the mathematics curriculum makes it mandatory that children accomplish every standard in the early numeracy continuum at the conceptual, procedural, and application levels. This means that teachers must become expert at using a variety of assessment tools, such as daily observation with recording, clinical interviews, performance tasks, daily work tasks, multiple-choice tests, student self-evaluation, and parent-teacher conferences, to continuously diagnose each child's strengths and weaknesses for every standard. When a deficit in concept or skill development is found, immediate interventions must be made to ensure that the child continues to make progress on that particular standard. Continuing to teach the prescribed curriculum to the child who is not making good progress is a guarantee of early learning failure. The shift must be away from just aligning curriculum, instruction, and assessment, toward aligning each child with appropriate curriculum, instruction, and assessment. It is simply not possible for a child to be successful in mathematics unless there is 100-percent accomplishment of all the standards. Each standard that a child fails to accomplish represents a gap in understanding and performance. The standards for the early years require that children work along a path of continuous progress and not become locked into a cycle of remediation and failure. Once a child has experienced early learning failure, setting that child on the road to success becomes a much more difficult task.

Most children come to school with an interest in numbers and how they are used in their everyday activities. It is our responsibility to build on those early experiences and ensure that children make continuous progress toward *every* standard set for the primary years. A child who exits the 2nd grade with good number sense and solid conceptual understanding of number concepts; and with computational and procedural fluency with addition, subtraction, and beginning multiplication; and who can apply those skills to solve problems is building toward success in algebra and, therefore, the opportunity to make life choices based on his or her academic strengths rather than weaknesses. Too many of our high school dropouts identify the reason for their dropout as their inability to make it through the mathematics requirements. Early learning failure has lifelong effects! Early learning success in mathematics is possible for most of our at-risk students. Quality instructional practices make the difference.

REFERENCES

Jensen, E. (1998). *Teaching with the brain in mind.* Alexandria, VA: Association for Supervision and Curriculum Development.

Meira, L. (1998). Making sense of instructional devices: The emergence of transparency in mathematical activity. *Journal for Research in Mathematics Education, 29*(2), 121–142.

National Council of Teachers of Mathematics (2000). *Principles and standards for school mathematics.* Reston, VA: Author.

Valencia, S. W., & Wixson, K. K. (1991). Diagnostic teaching. *Reading Teacher, 44,* 420–423.

Van de Walle, J. A. (1998). *Elementary and middle school mathematics: Teaching developmentally* (3rd ed.). New York: Longman.

WHO IS REALLY LEARNING DISABLED?

Gary L. Hessler

At a time when almost 50 percent of all special education students are considered to have a learning disability, some people are questioning whether students labeled learning disabled (LD) actually have a certifiable handicap (Spear-Swerling & Sternberg, 1996). According to critics, schools often label students as LD so that they may receive services exclusive to special education students, rather than because they are "really" LD. As these services increasingly rely on general school district revenues for funding, some think they are draining resources from students in the "regular" classroom.

The explanation for continuing rise in the percentage of students labeled LD can be found by looking at how schools typically provide remedial services to students in core areas such as reading and writing. Studies supported by the National Institute of Child Health and Human Development (NICHD; National Institutes of Health, Bethesda, Maryland) show that at least 20 to 30 percent of American students cannot read well enough to successfully complete schoolwork (Lyon, 1995a, 1997, 1998). Unfortunately, there are few remedial reading and writing services within regular education programs, especially at the middle and high school levels. The only remedial literacy services available are usually in special education programs, and students are often diagnosed as LD so that they may have access to these resources. Many of these students are not LD at all, however; some are learning English as a second language, while others are "curriculum casualties" who never received appropriate instruction in the first place (see Vellutino et al., 1996, 1997, 1998).

Students who are truly LD have cognitive, neurophysiological, and in many cases genetic disabilities (Lyon, 1995a; Vellutino et al., 1996, 1997). These difficulties typically last a lifetime, resist treatment, and require specialized instruction if the student is to make academic progress (Lyon 1995a, 1997; Shaywitz, 1996). While the actual percentage is unclear, approximately 5 percent of all students may be afflicted in this way (Torgesen, 2000); the other students identified as poor readers could improve their performance if they received more appropriately designed assessment and instruction, particularly in the early school years. Thus, most students who are at-risk can be brought up to grade level in reading and writing if they are identified early and receive carefully planned, direct, and systematic instruction in beginning reading and writing skills. This instruction usually emphasizes training in phonemic awareness and phonics skills, although the application of these skills in meaningful reading and writing activities is also important.

If cognitive and neurological learning disabilities truly exist, how can we identify them? This chapter explores the main characteristics of the LD student, as established by current research, in order to help readers develop an accurate, empirical understanding of learning disabilities.

Inherent in this discussion is the notion that educators must rethink the process by which children are currently characterized and identified as LD. There are certainly no definite answers, but a consideration of the empirically-based research data now available can have a profound effect on our understanding of the nature and characterization of LD, as well as on assessment and treatment policies and procedures. The premise is that poor and inappropriate parenting and education do not directly cause learning disabilities (Spear-Swerling & Sternberg, 1996, 1998). Those with learning disabilities come to school with actual and/or relative cognitive weaknesses that put them at risk for learning. However, support at home and at school can have a major impact—both positive and negative—on these children's learning. Even though these individuals are at risk when they arrive at school, the way in which the environment responds has a significant impact on whether learning is successful or not.

CURRENT EMPIRICAL KNOWLEDGE
ABOUT SPECIFIC LEARNING DISABILITIES

For the past 30 years or so, and particularly for the past 10 or 15 years, the NICHD has supported large-scale studies of individuals with learning disabilities (Lyon, 1995a). The studies are designed for independent replication and include prospective, longitudinal studies; intervention studies; neuro-imaging studies; and genetic studies. In all cases, researchers follow and evaluate large samples of students, and the findings are often independently validated at other NICHD sites. While the studies have historically emphasized reading, they have begun to focus on writing and mathematics. The following facts are based on the results of those studies, and represent the best empirical data currently available on learning disabilities.

Reading disabilities affect 20 to 30 percent of school-age children, or at least 15 million children. Reading ability varies from person to person along a continuous distribution. Children with poor reading skills do not represent a discrete entity separate from normal readers, but rather blend imperceptibly with normal readers along a continuum. Like obesity or hypertension, reading disabilities occur in varying degrees of severity, and there is no clear seam separating them from normal readers. Children with reading disabilities therefore do not represent a qualitatively different group of readers, but to varying degrees they are poor at skills necessary for proficient reading.

The relative frequency of reading problems is surprising: 20 to 30 percent of school age children have reading difficulties severe enough to hinder their performance in school (Lyon, 1995a, 1997, 1998). This is a large pool of potentially learning disabled students, and without changes to our current referral and diagnostic system, we can expect the number to continue rising. For more information, please see Capute, Accardo, and Shapiro (1994); Duane and Gray (1991); Lyon (1994, 1995a, 1997); Lyon, Gray, Karavagh, and Krasnegor (1993); and Shaywitz, Escobar, Shaywitz, Fletcher, and Makuch (1992).

Though schools identify approximately four times as many boys as girls as reading disabled, studies indicate that both are equally affected. According to research data, the referral and identification process for learning disabilities is gender biased. This may be because boys exhibit attention-deficit/hyperactivity disorders (ADHD) and other behavior problems more often than girls, and are therefore more likely to be referred for special services. There is also evidence that gender differences in brain organization make it easier for girls to compensate for reading disabilities. Nevertheless, the actual prevalence of reading disabilities is nearly identical in the two sexes. For more information, please see Capute, Accardo, and Shapiro (1994); Lyon (1995a); Lyon, Gray, Kavanagh, and Krasnegor (1993); Shaywitz (1996); and Shaywitz and Shaywitz (1996).

There is strong evidence for a neurobiological or genetic etiology of reading disabilities. Brain pathology and neuro-imaging studies indicate that people with reading disabilities have abnormalities in neuro-organization and function, predominately in or near the left temporal region of the brain. There is also strong evidence that reading disabilities are genetic, with deficits in phonological awareness showing the greatest heritability. For more information, please see Duane and Gray (1991); Lyon (1994, 1995a); Lyon et al. (1993); Richardson (1994); Shaywitz (1996); Shaywitz and Shaywitz (1996); and Torgesen (1995).

Reading disabilities, and learning disabilities in general, reflect a persistent deficit rather than a developmental lag. Approximately 74 percent of children who are reading disabled in the 3rd grade remain disabled in the 9th grade; few students independently outgrow a learning disability. Studies also show that reading disabilities persist into adulthood, and although some disabled students learn to read accurately, they continue to read slowly and nonautomatically. For more information, please see Lyon (1994, 1995a); Lyon et al. (1993); and Shaywitz (1996).

Attention-deficit/hyperactivity disorders (ADHD) and LD often coexist, but they are distinct disorders. ADHD is a neurobiological *behavior disorder,* and LD is a cognitive and neurobiological *learning disorder.* Children exhibit both disorders simultaneously in approximately 25 to 30 percent of LD cases. ADHD exacerbates the severity of LD by impeding the self-regulation, selective attention, and persistence that can otherwise help compensate for a learning disability. ADHD is more common among males, and because it often coexists with LD, boys are more likely than girls to be labeled learning disabled. For more information, please see Capute et al. (1994); Lyon (1995a); and Shaywitz, Fletcher, and Shaywitz (1995).

The best predictor of reading and writing disabilities in kindergarten and 1st grade is phonological awareness. The core deficits in reading and writing disabilities are in phonological awareness. Thus, measures that assess students' understanding of how words are composed of sounds that can be segmented and synthesized are robust predictors of students' reading and writing performance. Classroom observation as well as formal or informal assessment instruments that measure phonological awareness can be effectively used to identify those who are at risk for reading and writing disabilities. This is extremely important, since LD assessment should measure achievement skills as well as relevant domain-specific cognitive abilities (rather than global measures of IQ). Phonological awareness, for instance, should be measured and included in LD assessment, especially if the student is suspected of having a reading or writing disorder. For more information, please see Lyon (1994, 1995a); Lyon et al. (1993); Shaywitz (1996); Shaywitz and Shaywitz (1996); Torgesen (1995); and Torgesen and Wagner (1998).

Using an IQ–achievement discrepancy to identify individuals with LD appears to be invalid. Intelligence—i.e., higher level thinking, such as abstract reasoning and problem solving—is not related to phonological awareness. Thus, very intelligent students may experience learning disabilities, while less intelligent ones may be surprisingly good readers (decoders) or writers (spellers). Furthermore, LD students have similar information processing, genetic, and neurophysiological profiles whether they display IQ–achievement discrepancies or not. Although IQ may foretell some aspects of academic performance, such as reading comprehension, mathematical reasoning, and meaningful written expression, it is not a good predictor of specific learning disabilities, because most learning problems are due to deficiencies in automaticity, rapid serial word naming, and phonological processing, rather than abstract reasoning and problem solving. For more information, please see Aaron (1997); Fletcher et al. (1998); Lyon (1994, 1995a, 1995b); Lyon et al. (1993); Share and Stanovich (1995); Shaywitz (1996); Shaywitz and Shaywitz (1996); Siegel (1988, 1998); and Spear-Swerling and Sternberg (1998).

Writing backwards and reversing letters and words are not necessarily symptoms of reading and writing disabilities. Writing backwards and reversing letters and words are common to all children in the early stages of reading and writing development. Students with actual disabilities often have problems naming letters and words, but not necessarily copying them. Since reading and writing disabilities usually reflect a deficit in phonological—rather than visual—processing, there is scant evidence that the disabilities would be alleviated by visual training. For more information, please see Berninger (1998, 1999); Lyon (1994); Lyon et al. (1993); and Shaywitz (1996).

Due to deficiencies in phonological awareness, most disabled students do not readily acquire phonics when learning to read and write. Students who exhibit phonological awareness understand that spoken words are composed of individual sounds. In order to decode single words accurately, students must first be able to segment words and syllables into abstract constituent units of sound (phonemes). This ability is the foundation for beginning reading (phonics) and writing (spelling), and its absence is the source of most reading and writing difficulties:

> Children and adults with reading disability have difficulties with the most basic step in the reading pathway: breaking down the written word into simpler phonological units. As a result of this deficit, children cannot break the reading code. The discovery of the phonological basis of reading disability allows us to understand why even some very bright in-

dividuals cannot learn to read. Thus, although other components of the language system, such as higher-order language processes involved in reading comprehension and meaning are generally not impaired in reading disability, individuals with reading disability cannot access or use these higher-order skills until they have translated words into their phonological forms. The phonological model crystallizes exactly what a reading disability involves: children with good intelligence who cannot use their often excellent higher-order neurolinguistic and cognitive skills, because of a block in the first step of the reading pathway (Shaywitz & Shaywitz, 1996, p. 258).

Berninger (1998, 1999) proposes a similar model for writing disorders that involves impaired phonological and orthographic processing and fine motor abilities, as well as handwriting and spelling difficulties that constrict meaningful writing. For more information, please see Berninger (1998, 1999); Honig (1996); Lyon (1994, 1995a); Shaywitz (1996); Shaywitz and Shaywitz (1996); Snider (1995); Torgesen (1995); and Torgesen and Wagner (1998).

The ability to read and write depends on the automatic recognition and spelling of single words. Fluent readers and writers accurately and automatically identify and retrieve the spelling of words, which permits them to concentrate on comprehension and meaning when reading and writing. Most disabled readers and writers, however, cannot accurately and automatically identify or spell words. They must concentrate on word recognition and spelling, which interferes with their ability to comprehend what they're reading—even if they can identify enough words to understand the material—and to write in a meaningful manner. For more information, please see Berninger (1998, 1999); Foorman (1995); Graham (1999); Honig (1996); Lyon (1994, 1995a); Moats (1995); and Shaywitz (1996).

Teachers must present disabled readers and writers with highly structured, explicit, and intensive instruction in the rules of phonics and in their application to print. Studies show that systematic, structured phonics instruction for students with reading and writing disabilities is more effective than meaning-based teaching devoid of phonics; in fact, perhaps 50 to 70 percent of students appear to learn to read and write regardless of the instructional approach (Honig, 1996; Lyon, 1997, 1998). These students can apparently intuit the skills necessary for proficient reading and writing even if educators do not directly teach them the skills. In contrast, students with weak cognitive processes—due either to cognitive disorders or to a lack of relevant preschool experiences—must be taught directly, because they cannot infer the rules of phonics through exposure to written material. For more information, please see Adams (1990); Beck and Juel (1995); Berninger (1998, 1999); Foorman (1995); Foorman, Francis, Shaywitz, Shaywitz, and Fletcher (1997); Foorman, Francis, Fletcher, Schatschneider, and Mehta (1998); Graham (1999); Honig (1996); Lyon (1994, 1995a); Shaywitz (1996); Torgesen (1995); Torgesen and Wagner (1998); Torgesen (1997); Vellutino, Scanlon, and Sipay (1997); and Vellutino et al. (1996).

Effective reading and writing instruction for LD children involves a balanced program of basic skills and meaningful activities *presented at each student's achievement level.* Educators must teach to the student's present performance level and target deficient skills, a task which usually requires intensive instruction in phonological awareness and phonics. Teachers must also provide opportunities to practice applying the skills in meaningful situations. A balanced program combines the language-rich activities of reading and writing—which are aimed at enhancing meaning and understanding—with the explicit instruction in skills necessary for developing fluency with print, such as phonological awareness and phonics skills, the automatic recognition of words, and the ability to decode, write, and spell (Honig, 1996). For more information, please see Adams (1990); Adams and Bruck (1995); Berninger (1998, 1999); Graham (1999); Honig (1996); and Lyon et al. (1997).

Early intervention in kindergarten and 1st grade is our best hope for alleviating reading and writing difficulties. Children with reading disabilities in the later elementary grades appear to require much more intensive instruction, in smaller groups and for a longer time, than do students whose disabilities are identified by the 1st grade. Older students with disabilities often have negative attitudes about reading and writing that are difficult to eradicate. Intervening early and intensively with at-risk students is best, from both economic and humane perspectives. For example, early intervention can result in the alleviation of many reading and writing problems, thus avoiding many of the personal problems associated with reading and writing disabilities in our society. It can also help avoid the later need for more expensive special education services. For more information, please see Fletcher et al. (1998); Lyon (1997, 1998); Richardson (1994); Torgesen (1998); Torgesen, Wagner, Rashotte, Alexander, and Conway (1997); Vellutino et al. (1996, 1997); and Vellutino, Scanlon, and Tanzman (1998).

Below are some examples of the relationship between relevant domain-specific cognitive abilities and academic achievement. A domain-specific cognitive ability is one which is relatively independent of other cognitive skills, and is associated with the development of various areas of academic achievement. (Phonological awareness, for instance). For more information, please see Berninger (1998, 1999); Fletcher et al. (1998); McGrew (1993); McGrew and Hessler (1995); McGrew and Knopik (1993); Shaywitz and Shaywitz (1996); Spear-Swerling and Sternberg (1998); Torgesen and Wagner (1998); and Vellutino et al. (1994).

• **Basic Reading Skills.** Phonological awareness, rapid serial word naming, and processing speed (automaticity) are necessary, but not sufficient, for fluent basic reading skills. Fluent basic reading skills are necessary, but not sufficient, for proficient reading comprehension.

• **Reading Comprehension.** Fluent basic reading skills, working memory, verbal comprehension and reasoning, and fluid reasoning (i.e., abstract, creative thinking) are necessary, but not sufficient, for proficient reading comprehension.

• **Basic Mathematics Skills.** Processing speed (automaticity) is necessary, but not sufficient, for fluent basic mathematics skills. Fluent basic mathematics skills are necessary, but not sufficient, for proficient mathematics reasoning.

• **Mathematical Reasoning.** Fluent basic mathematics skills, working memory, verbal comprehension and reasoning, and fluid reasoning are necessary, but not sufficient, for proficient mathematical reasoning.

• **Basic Writing Skills.** Phonological awareness, processing speed (automaticity), orthographic processing, and fine motor abilities are necessary, but not sufficient, for fluent basic writing skills. Fluent basic writing skills are necessary, but not sufficient, for proficient meaningful written expression.

• **Meaningful Written Expression.** Fluent basic writing skills, working memory, verbal comprehension and reasoning, and fluid reasoning are necessary, but not sufficient, for proficient meaningful written expression.

CHARACTERISTICS OF THE LEARNING DISABLED

Given the best available empirical data, how can we characterize specific learning disabilities? Here is an operational definition:

> Specific learning disabilities are of a neuro-biological or genetic origin characterized by difficulties with basic reading skills, reading comprehension, basic mathematics skills, mathematical reasoning, basic writing skills, or meaningful writing that significantly interfere with

learning and performance. These difficulties reflect central processing disorders and are unexpected in relation to age, cognitive abilities, or other academic abilities. They are not the direct result of mental impairment, sensory impairment, or insufficient or inappropriate instruction.

This definition differs considerably from previous definitions. First, it does not mention the need for a discrepancy between intellectual ability and academic achievement. There is little, if any, evidence that such a discrepancy must be present in order for an LD diagnosis. *Requiring this sort of discrepancy delays the identification of LD, fails to indicate whether or not a learning disability exists, fails to indicate the cognitive basis for LD, and fails to provide information about appropriate instructional strategies and procedures* (Aaron, 1997; Fletcher et al., 1998; Lyon, 1995a, 1995b; Share & Stanovich, 1995; Siegel, 1988, 1998; Spear-Swerling & Sternberg, 1996, 1998). Measuring intellectual abilities is sometimes important, however, because data about a student's verbal comprehension and reasoning can help determine the cognitive basis for problems with reading comprehension, mathematical reasoning, and meaningful writing. By studying cognitive assessment data, educators can discern the nature, course, and treatment of a student's disabilities, rather than simply indicating whether student achievement is commensurate with intellectual ability.

Second, the original definition of LD does not distinguish between basic writing skills and meaningful writing (Federal Register, 1977; United States Office of Education, 1977). Prevailing evidence suggests that most writing disabilities are due to problems with basic writing skills—particularly lack of fluency and automaticity with handwriting and spelling—and not with ideation or higher-level writing ability (Berninger, 1998, 1999; Graham, 1999).

Third, I have not included listening comprehension or oral expression in my definition. These are important dimensions of performance, but they are considered in definitions of speech and language impairments. In addition, listening comprehension is often considered a central processing ability, and, indeed, it is sometimes used to measure expectancy, rather than achievement, in reading comprehension (Aaron, 1989, 1991; Fletcher et al., 1998).

Finally, I have dramatically changed the exclusionary criteria for LD in the present definition. It is often extremely difficult to isolate the effects of economic, social, or cultural factors on learning. Such a task is required in existing LD definitions, so that educators do not inappropriately identify disadvantaged students, or those from different social or cultural backgrounds, as learning disabled. In my definition, a student with a cognitive disorder, who has had appropriate instruction and reasonable exposure to the prevailing language and culture for a reasonable amount of time, should be seen as possibly learning disabled. As Lyon (1995b) notes,

> To date the majority of definitions for dyslexia have relied heavily on numerous exclusionary criteria. . . . Given the primary role of these exclusion statements in the identification of dyslexia individuals, children have been frequently diagnosed on the basis of what they were not, rather than what they were. . . . It is now clear, however, that excluding children from the diagnosis of dyslexia because of cultural differences, inadequate instruction, or co-morbid attentional, social, and behavioral deficits has no empirical basis. . . . (pp. 17–18).

Identification of LD is a systemic issue, fundamentally based on the availability of relevant intensive instruction for all students, so that most will flourish and only those with relatively severe, cognitively-based learning disorders will need special identification and support. Figure 4.1 shows my proposed specific criteria for identifying LD students who qualify for special education services. Educators can use these criteria to identify any student with cognitively-based learning disorders. Such assessment is especially important because, as I emphasized earlier, learning problems occur along a continuum of severity on which there is no clear seam (Shaywitz et al., 1992). Typically, schools reserve special education services for the most severe learning problems, which my proposed definition and criteria will help identify. The criteria are also appropriate for identifying less severe cases, depending on the school's cut-off point for academic achievement. I'll briefly review the criteria below.

• **Learning disabled students display neither primary mental retardation nor a sensory impairment (i.e., visual or hearing impairment).** A student with mental retardation or severe vision or hearing difficulties might have trouble learning, at least through traditional instruction, but such a student would not necessarily have a specific learning disability. The presence of additional handicaps such as emotional disturbance or physical impairments should not preclude the consideration of learning disabilities. Therefore, a student could be certified with both an emotional disturbance *and* a learning disability. If children can have both ADHD and LD, or language impairment and LD, then dual certification in other areas should be considered as well, if cognitively-based learning problems are present.

• **Learning disabled students have received adequate educational opportunities, and they have not responded well to early intervention**

FIGURE 4.1
WHO, THEN, IS REALLY LD?

- Students who are neither mentally retarded nor sensory impaired
- Students who have received adequate educational opportunities and have resisted early intervention
- Students who cannot successfully perform in regular education settings without special education support
- Students whose academic difficulties are unexpected in relation to their age, cognitive abilities, or other academic abilities
- Students with severe deficits in basic reading skills, reading comprehension, mathematic skills, mathematics reasoning, basic writing skills, or meaningful writing associated with relevant cognitive difficulties.

strategies that are typically successful with struggling students. Educators should actively implement early identification strategies so that all at-risk learners can be identified as early as possible. Educators should also provide appropriate intervention strategies at the earliest sign of a deficit or problem, typically through intensive instruction in phonological awareness and in phonics activities associated with meaningful reading and writing activities. Teachers should also monitor student progress throughout the intervention process to determine whether instruction is effective or more explicit instruction is needed. As Lyon (1997, 1998) notes, well-trained teachers can help 85 to 95 percent of poor readers in kindergarten and 1st grade raise their reading skills to average levels through combined instruction in phoneme awareness, phonics, and reading fluency and comprehension. If, however, intervention is delayed until even the age of nine, approximately 75 percent of disabled students will continue to have difficulties learning to read. According to Vellutino et al. (1996, 1997, 1998), early intervention helps distinguish between those with learning problems due to "experiential/instructional deficits" and those with "basic cognitive deficits"; they also note that "most children who might have been classified as 'learning disabled' prior to intervention would not have been classified following intervention" (1997, p. 370).

Almost all school districts have now incorporated "prereferral" procedures in their systems. The effectiveness of these efforts varies depending on a number of factors; in many schools, they are not considered in a serious manner and are of limited effectiveness. Many regular education teachers see the prereferral process as an unnecessary hoop to be jumped through before a child can be referred for special education. I suggest that all students be carefully assessed and monitored, particularly in kindergarten and 1st grade, so that they can receive appropriate and increasingly intense instruction if they are not learning. If legitimate and appropriate regular educational alternatives are not successful, children would then be considered potential LD students. In this sense, the indication that a student is resistant to typically successful early intervention procedures is a strong sign that a more severe form of a specific cognitively-based learning disability exists.

• **Learning disabled students cannot successfully learn or perform in regular education settings without special education support, i.e., that they have severe academic difficulties that have been documented.** If the student has already met the two previous criteria, educators can usually document that the student meets this one also. Given the fiscal realities of providing special education, however, many schools may establish a cut-off point for special education services to limit enrollment. For instance, some experts believe that LD in its most severe form involves the bottom 3 to 5 percent of the general population (Torgesen, 2000). A district might therefore determine this percentage of the student body to be the limit for admission to special education services.

• **Learning disabled students have academic difficulties that are unexpected in relation to their age, cognitive abilities, or other academic abilities.** Traditionally, this unexpectedness has been determined through the use of the IQ–achievement discrepancy model described earlier, which is a generally invalid model. There are other ways to accurately show discrepancies, however. Evidence of unexpected variation could include academic achievement below age or grade levels (age- or grade-based discrepancy), significant variation in cognitive performance (intra-cognitive discrepancy), or significant variation in academic achievement (intra-achievement discrepancy).

• **Learning disabled students have a severe deficit in basic reading skills, reading comprehension, basic mathematics skills, mathematical reasoning, basic writing skills, or meaningful written expression that is associated with relevant cognitive difficulties.** This criterion is important because certain domain-specific cognitive abilities appear to be related to academic achievement. Assessment of these deficits should focus on the evaluation of academic achievement and related cognitive skills, and has direct implications for early intervention and instruction; a student with cognitive difficulties and associated academic achievement problems probably has a cognitively-based learning disability. For more information, please see

Fletcher et al. (1998); Share and Stanovich (1995); Spear-Swerling and Sternberg (1998); Torgesen and Wagner (1998); and Vellutino et al. (1997).

CONCLUSION

I have characterized reading and writing learning disabilities in this chapter according to the best available contemporary information. However, as anyone involved in this field can see, the definition and criteria are still in some respects problematic. For example, we still do not know how severe cognitive processes need to be to interfere with learning, or what cut-off points for academic achievement schools should establish before labeling a child learning disabled (Fletcher et al., 1998). Nevertheless, I believe my definition represents an improvement over previous definitions, because it permits earlier identification of learning disabilities, which is consistent with research suggesting that early intervention is optimal. Certainly, continued research in this field will help us refine this definition to more effectively meet the needs of the learning disabled.

REFERENCES

Aaron, P. G. (1989). *Dyslexia and hyperlexia: Diagnosis and management of developmental reading disabilities.* Boston: Kluwer Academic Publishers.

Aaron, P. G. (1991). Can reading disabilities be diagnosed without using intelligence tests? *Journal of Learning Disabilities, 24,* 178–186, 191.

Aaron, P. G. (1997). The impending demise of the discrepancy formula. *Review of Educational Research, 67,* 461–502.

Adams, J. J. (1990). *Beginning to read: Thinking and learning about print.* Cambridge, MA: MIT Press.

Adams, M. J., & Bruck, M. (1995, Summer). Resolving the "Great Debate." *American Educator, 19*(2), 7–20.

Beck, I. L., & Juel, C. (1995, Summer). The role of decoding in learning to read. *American Educator, 19*(2), 8, 21–25, 39–42.

Berninger, V. W. (1998). *Process assessment of the learner: Guidelines for intervention.* San Antonio, TX: The Psychological Corporation.

Berninger, V. W. (1999). Coordinating transcription and text generation in working memory during composing: Automatic and constructive processes. *Learning Disability Quarterly, 22,* 99–112.

Capute, A. J., Accardo, P. J., & Shapiro B. K. (Eds.). (1994). *Learning disabilities spectrum: ADD, ADHD, and LD.* Baltimore: York Press, Inc.

Duane, D. D., & Gray, D. B. (Eds.). (1991). *The reading brain: The biological basis of dyslexia.* Baltimore: York Press, Inc.

Federal Register (1977, December 29) (65082–65085), Washington, DC.

Fletcher, J. M., Francis, D. J., Shaywitz, S. E., Lyon, G. R., Foorman, B. R., Stuebing, K. K., & Shaywitz, B. A. (1998). Intelligent testing and the discrepancy model for children with learning disabilities. *Learning Disabilities Research and Practice, 13,* 186–203.

Foorman, B. R. (1995). Research on "The Great Debate": Code-oriented versus whole language approaches to reading instruction: *School Psychology Review, 24,* 376–392.

Foorman, B. R., Francis, D. J., Fletcher, J. M., Schatschneider, C., & Mehta, P. (1998). The role of instruction in learning to read: Preventing reading failure in at-risk children. *Journal of Educational Psychology, 90*(1), 37–55.

Foorman, B. R., Francis, D. J., Shaywitz, S. E., Shaywitz, B. A., & Fletcher, J. M. (1997). The case for early reading intervention. In B.Blackman (Ed.), *Foundations of reading acquisition and dyslexia: Implications for early intervention* (pp. 243–264). Mahwah, NJ: Lawrence Erlbaum Associates.

Graham, S. (1999). Handwriting and spelling instruction for students with learning disabilities: A review. *Learning Disability Quarterly, 22,* 78–98.

Honig, B. (1996). *Teaching our children to read: The role of skills in a comprehensive reading program.* Thousand Oaks, CA: Corwin Press, Inc.

Lyon, G. R. (Ed.). (1994). *Frames of reference for the assessment of learning disabilities: New views on measurement issues.* Baltimore: Paul H. Brookes Publishing Company.

Lyon, G. R. (1995a). Research initiatives in learning disabilities from scientists supported by the National Institute of Child Health and Human Development. *Journal of Child Neurology, 10*(1), 120–126.

Lyon, G. R. (1995b). Toward a definition of dyslexia. *Annuals of Dyslexia, 45,* 3–27.

Lyon, G. R. (1997). Report on learning disabilities research. Testimony given before the Committee on Education and the Workforce in the U.S. House of Representatives, July 10, 1997. (Available online at www.1donline.org).

Lyon, G. R. (1998). Report on learning disabilities research supported by the National Institute of Child Health and Human Development. Address to the Committee of Labor and Human Resources of the U.S. Senate, April 28, 1998. (Available online at: www.rlac.com/edarticles.htm).

Lyon, G. R., Alexander, D., & Yaffe, S. (1997). Progress and promise in research on learning disabilities. *Learning Disabilities: A Multi-Disciplinary Journal, 8,* 1–6.

Lyon, G. R., Gray, D. B., Kavanagh, J. F., & Krasnegor, N. A. (Eds.). (1993). *Better understanding learning disabilities: New views from research and their implications for education and public policies.* Baltimore: Paul H. Brookes Publishing Company.

McGrew, K. S. (1993). The relationship between the WJ-R Gf-Gc cognitive clusters and reading achievement across the lifespan. *Journal of Psychoeducational Assessment* (Monograph Series: WJ-R Monograph), 39–53.

McGrew, K. S., & Hessler, G. L. (1995). The relationship between the WJ-R Gf-Gc cognitive clusters and mathematics achievement across the life-span. *Journal of Psychoeducational Assessment, 13,* 21–38.

McGrew, K. S., & Knopik, S. N. (1993). The relationship between the WJ-R Gf-Gc cognitive clusters and writing achievement across the life-span. *School Psychology Review, 22,* 687–695.

Moats, L. C. (1995). *Spelling: Development, disability, and instruction.* Baltimore: York Press, Inc.

Richardson, S. O. (1994). *Doctors ask questions about dyslexia: A review of medical research*. Baltimore: The International Dyslexia Association.

Share, D. L., & Stanovich, K. E. (1995). Cognitive processes in early reading development: Accommodating individual differences into a model of acquisition. *Issues in Education, 1,* 1–57.

Shaywitz, B. A., Fletcher, J. M., & Shaywitz, S. E. (1995). Defining and classifying learning disabilities and attention deficit hyperactivity disorder. *Journal of Child Neurology, 10,* 50–57.

Shaywitz, S. E. (1996). Dyslexia. *Scientific American, 275*(5), 98–104

Shaywitz, S. E., Escobar, M. D., Shaywitz, B. A., Fletcher, J. M., & Makuch, R. (1992). Evidence that dyslexia may represent the lower tail of a normal distribution of reading ability. *The New England Journal of Medicine, 326,* 145–150.

Shaywitz, S. E., & Shaywitz, B. A. (1996). Unlocking learning disabilities: The neurological basis. In S. C. Cramer & W. Ellis (Eds.), *Learning disabilities: Lifelong issues* (pp. 255–260). Baltimore: Paul H. Brookes Publishing Company.

Siegel, L. S. (1988). Evidence IQ scores are irrelevant to the definition and analysis of reading disability. *Canadian Journal of Psychology, 42,* 201–215.

Siegel, L. S. (1998). The discrepancy formula: Its use and abuse. In B. K. Shapiro, P. J. Accardo, & A. J. Capute (Eds.), *Specific reading disability: A view of the spectrum* (pp. 123–135). Baltimore: York Press, Inc.

Snider, V. E. (1995). A primer of phonemic awareness: What it is, why it's important, and how to teach it. *School Psychology Review, 24,* 443–455.

Spear-Swerling, L., & Sternberg, R. J. (1996). *Off-track: When poor readers become "learning disabled."* Boulder, CO: Westview Press.

Spear-Swerling, L., & Sternberg, R. J. (1998). Curing our "epidemic" of learning disabilities. *Phi Delta Kappan, 79*(5), 397–401.

Torgesen, J. K. (1995). *Phonological Awareness: A critical factor in dyslexia*. Baltimore: The International Dyslexia Association.

Torgesen, J. K. (1998). Catch them before they fall. *American Educator, 22*(1–2), 32–39.

Torgesen, J. K. (2000). Individual differences in response to early interventions in reading: The lingering problem of treatment resisters. *Learning Disabilities Research and Practice, 15,* 55–64.

Torgesen, J. K., & Wagner, R. K. (1998). Alternative diagnostic approaches to specific developmental reading disabilities. *Learning Disabilities Research and Practice, 13,* 220–232.

Torgesen, J. K., Wagner, R. K., & Rashotte, C. A. (1997). Approaches to the prevention and remediation of phonologically based reading disabilities. In B. Blackman (Ed.), *Foundations of reading acquisition and dyslexia: Implications for early intervention* (pp. 287–304). Mahwah, NJ: Lawrence Erlbaum Associates.

Torgesen, J. K., Wagner, R. K., Rashotte, C. A., Alexander, A. W., & Conway, T. (1997). Preventative and remedial interventions for children with severe reading disabilities. *Learning Disabilities: A Multi-Disciplinary Journal, 8,* 51–62.

United States Office of Education. (1977). Assistance to states for education for handicapped children: Procedures for evaluating specific learning disabilities. *Federal Register, 42,* G1082–G1085.

Vellutino, F. R., Scanlon, D. M., & Sipay, E. R. (1997). Toward distinguishing between cognitive and experiential deficits as primary sources of difficulty in learning to read: The importance of early intervention in diagnosing specific reading disability. In B. Blackman (Ed.), *Foundations of reading acquisition and dyslexia: Implications for early intervention* (pp. 347–379). Mahwah, NJ: Lawrence Erlbaum Associates.

Vellutino, F. R., Scanlon, D. M., Sipay, E. R., Small, S. G., Pratt, A., Chen, R., & Denckla, M. B. (1996). Cognitive profiles of difficult to remediate and readily remediated poor readers: Early intervention as a vehicle for distinguishing between cognitive and experiential deficits as basic causes of specific reading disability. *Journal of Educational Psychology, 88*(4), 601–638.

Vellutino, F. R., Scanlon, D. M., & Tanzman, M. S. (1994). Components of reading ability: Issues and problems in operationalizing word identification, phonological coding, and orthographic coding. In G. R. Lyon (Ed.), *Frames of reference for the assessment of learning disabilities: New views on measurement issues* (pp. 279–324). Baltimore: Paul H. Brookes Publishing Company.

Vellutino, F. R., Scanlon, D. M., & Tanzman, M. S. (1998). The case for early intervention in diagnosing specific reading disability. *Journal of School Psychology, 36,* 367–397.

ENHANCING THE LISTENING ENVIRONMENT FOR EARLY LEARNING SUCCESS

Carol Flexer

F avorable listening environments at home and at school provide a clear auditory pathway to the child's brain. In order for critical auditory brain tissue to grow, the brain must receive ongoing detailed auditory input. This chapter describes how to enhance acoustic accessibility for children in order to stimulate auditory brain growth that will serve as the foundation for learning success.

AUDITORY BRAIN DEVELOPMENT

Studies in brain development show that sensory stimulation of the auditory centers of the brain is critically important and influences the actual organization of auditory brain pathways (Boothroyd, 1997; Chermak & Musiek, 1997; Musiek & Berge, 1998). The same brain areas—the primary and secondary auditory areas—are most active when a child listens and when a child reads. That is, phonological or phonemic awareness, which is the explicit awareness of the speech sound structure of language units, forms the basis for the development of reading skills (Gilbertson & Bramlett, 1998). The point is that anything we can do to "program" those critical and powerful auditory centers of the brain with acoustic detail will expand children's opportunities and contribute to early learning success (Robertson, 2000). The checklist of strategies in Figure 5.1 will help parents and teachers promote auditory learning with subsequent auditory brain growth.

FIGURE 5.1
HOW PARENTS AND TEACHERS CAN PROVIDE ACTIVE LISTENING
AND AUDITORY-BASED LANGUAGE ENRICHMENT

1. The quieter the room and the closer you are to your child, the better you will be heard. Remember, your child may have difficulty "overhearing" conversations and hearing you from a distance. You need to be close to your child when you speak. Your child's brain needs constant, detailed auditory input in order to develop.

2. Focus on listening, not just seeing. Call attention to sounds and to conversations in the room.

3. Maintain a joint focus of attention when reading and when engaged in activities. That is, the child looks at the book or at the activity while listening to you.

4. Speak in sentences, not single words, with clear speech and using lots of melody.

5. Read aloud to your child daily. Infants can be read to, not just older children. Investigate the children's literature that would be appropriate for your child's age and interests. Infants and children who are read aloud to, early and often, tend to be successful readers.

6. Sing or read nursery rhymes to your baby or young child every day. Nursery rhymes and songs assist in the development of phonemic awareness—the explicit awareness of the speech sound structure of language units that forms the basis for the development of reading skills.

7. Name objects in the environment as you encounter them during daily routines. Be mindful constantly of expanding vocabulary. Without vocabulary, reading comprehension is impossible.

8. Talk about and describe how things sound, look, and feel. Knowledge of how the world works is basic to reading comprehension.

9. Talk about where objects are located. Use many prepositions such as in, on, under, behind, beside, next to, and between. Knowledge of prepositions is important for following directions and for bridging concrete to abstract thinking.

10. Compare how objects or actions are similar and different in size, shape, quantity, smell, color, and texture.

11. Describe sequences. Talk about the steps involved in activities as you are doing the activity. Sequencing assists in organizing thinking and in expanding auditory memory.

12. Tell familiar stories or stories about events from your day or from your past. Keep narratives simpler for younger children and increase complexity as your child grows.

HEARING PROBLEMS

Hearing problems, whether caused by ear infections or a poor acoustic learning environment, can negatively affect the development of a child's auditory brain centers, with subsequent deficits in spoken language, reading and writing skills, and academic performance (Flexer, 1999). That is, hearing problems can be described as an invisible acoustic filter that distorts, smears, or eliminates incoming sounds, especially sounds from a distance—even a short distance. The negative effects of a hearing problem may be apparent, but the hearing problem itself is invisible and easily ignored or underestimated.

Children with hearing problems cannot receive intelligible speech well over distances. This reduction in earshot has tremendous consequences for life and classroom performance because distance hearing is linked to passive/casual/incidental listening and learning. Also, the farther away any child is from the desired sound source (typically the teacher), the weaker the signal and the poorer the intelligibility of the spoken message.

There is a big difference between an "audible" signal and an "intelligible" signal. Speech is audible if the person is able simply to detect its presence. However, for speech to be intelligible, the child must be able to discriminate the word-sound distinctions of individual phonemes or speech sounds. When speech is audible but not consistently intelligible, children may hear, for example, words such as "walked," "walking," "walker," and "walks" all as "__ah."

It seems that children ought to know when they are missing verbal information, but that's not the case. The problem is that you don't know that you didn't hear it—because you didn't hear it! Moreover, most children (and adults too) may not know that they "misheard" a message unless they already have had experience with the language and topic under discussion. Consequently, children often have an unrealistic perception of the amount and accuracy of the information that they are receiving from the environment. So even if a teacher asks, "Are you hearing me?" children almost always will say "Yes." How can a child estimate the quantity and quality of the information that he or she did *not* hear accurately?

Children are not short adults—and children do not listen the way adults do for two main reasons. First, the auditory neurological network in children is not fully developed until a child is about 15 years old. Second, children do not bring 30-plus years of listening and life experience to a learning situation. Consequently, children cannot perform the automatic "auditory/cognitive closure" of missed information like adults. To fill in the blanks of missed information, that information must already be in the brain's data banks for retrieval. Children, therefore, need a sharper auditory signal than adults. That is, a classroom might sound fine to an adult but be woefully inadequate for typical children who are not neurologically developed and who do not have decades of language and life experience. Because hearing is a first-order event in a mainstream classroom, if children do not hear clearly and consistently, their academic potential is compromised.

ACOUSTIC ACCESSIBILITY IN THE CLASSROOM

There is a direct relationship between hearing and learning. Because mainstreamed classrooms are auditory-verbal environments, listening is the primary modality for learning. Children must have clear and consistent access to spoken instruction, or the entire premise of the educational system is undermined (Berg, 1987).

The quieter the learning environment, the better acoustic access there is to a child's brain. There are three basic factors to consider in creating a quiet room: ambient (surrounding or background) noise level, reverberation (echo), and signal-to-noise ratio (S/N ratio).

The ambient noise level typically is measured with a sound level meter in an unoccupied classroom. Ambient noise in the classroom can originate from sources outside the classroom or even from sources outside the building, especially if doors and windows are open or were not installed to be acoustic barriers. Outside sources can include traffic noise, lawn equipment, air conditioners or heating systems, playground noise, and general environmental street noise. Inside noises can originate from children, equipment, computers, heating and cooling systems, ducts, fluorescent lighting systems with faulty ballasts, mechanical devices of any kind, music, etc. The greater the ambient noise level, the more difficult it is for children to hear clearly.

Reverberation refers to the echo caused by sound being reflected off smooth surfaces such as walls, ceilings, windows, tables, and chalkboards. Large rooms with high ceilings, bare walls, and bare floors tend to be highly reverberant environments. The longer the reverberation time, the more difficult it is for children to hear clearly.

Signal-to-noise ratio (S/N ratio) is the relationship between the desired auditory signal, typically the teacher's speech, and all unwanted background sounds. The more favorable the S/N ratio, the clearer and more intelligible the speech signal received by the pupils in the classroom.

In 1995, the American Speech-Language-Hearing Association (ASHA) recommended the following acoustic guidelines for classrooms:

1. Ambient noise level in an unoccupied classroom should not be louder than 30 to 35 dBA (a measure of intensity of sound).

2. Reverberation time should not exceed 0.4 seconds.

3. The S/N ratio should not be poorer than +15 dB (a measure of intensity).

Our goal should be to ensure the quietest learning environments possible by:

- Using acoustical ceiling tile.
- Carpeting floors or using some form of rubber tip or tennis balls on the legs of desks and chairs.
- Hanging thick curtains or drapes.
- Keeping fluorescent lighting systems and ventilating systems in good repair.
- Having well-fitting doors and windows and keeping them closed.
- Keeping children and instruction away from noise sources.
- Having a small class size.
- Having one activity occurring at a time, with no acoustic "spillage" from other activities.
- Having one acoustic focus in a room.
- Avoiding all open-plan classrooms.

Sadly, despite information about the necessity of having a favorable classroom environment, most classrooms continue to remain acoustically hostile (Crandell & Smaldino, 1994). Classrooms require attention to their acoustic environment in addition to the installation of soundfield systems in order to meet the recommended acoustic guidelines (Berg, 1993).

SOUNDFIELD AMPLIFICATION: FM OR INFRARED

Once in a while, a simple and straightforward possibility occurs that can make a profound difference in people's lives. This chapter features such a startling possibility for children's classroom learning: soundfield amplification.

For the past 15 years, the author has been involved personally with quantitative and qualitative research concerning soundfield amplification—traveling extensively around the country; observing classrooms; talking with teachers, audiologists, speech-language pathologists, parents, and children; and presenting training workshops about soundfield technology. These experiences have led to the conclusion that soundfield systems can, in fact, make a huge difference in the learning environment, and thus in the learning potential of children. Soundfield technology can create an acoustic medium in the classroom for the delivery of knowledge.

Specifically, a soundfield amplification system is similar to a small, high-fidelity, wireless, public address system that is self-contained in a classroom. The teacher wears a small, unobtrusive wireless microphone so that teacher mobility is not restricted. His or her speech is sent from the microphone through a transmitter to a receiver, where it is delivered to the students through several loudspeakers—usually four (Crandell, Smoldino, & Flexer, 1995).

Soundfield amplification can use FM or infrared technology. FM is a term applied to the radio transmission of signals, and infrared systems use the transmission medium of invisible light. Both systems amplify the teacher's voice throughout the classroom, thereby providing a clear and consistent signal to all pupils in the room no matter where they or the teacher are located. The positioning of the remote microphone close to the mouth of the teacher or other desired sound source creates a favorable S/N ratio and a clearer spoken message.

When properly adjusted, the system can counteract weak teacher voice levels and overcome background noise by increasing the overall speech level and producing a nearly uniform speech level throughout the room (Flexer, Millin, & Brown, 1990). There is never a "back-row effect" in a properly amplified classroom; every child hears as if seated in a front-row center seat.

CHILDREN WHO WOULD BENEFIT MOST
FROM AN AMPLIFIED CLASSROOM

Virtually all children could benefit from soundfield systems because the improved S/N ratio creates a more favorable learning environment. If children could hear better, more clearly, and more consistently, they would have an opportunity to learn more efficiently.

The following populations seem to be especially in need of this technology:

1. Children with fluctuating conductive hearing impairments, primarily caused by ear infections or ear wax, represent a large population of

children. One-fourth to one-third of typical kindergarten and 1st-grade children do not hear normally on any given day (Flexer, Richards, Buie, & Brandy, 1994; Ray, Sarff, & Glassford, 1984). In fact, a recent study found that at least seven million school children have some degree of hearing impairment that will compromise their learning potential (Niskar et al., 1998). Therefore, if all classrooms in a district cannot be amplified at the same time, it seems reasonable to amplify preschool, kindergarten, and 1st-through 3rd-grade classrooms before amplifying middle and secondary school classrooms, because the ability to hear word and sound distinctions is a primary basis for the development of academic competencies (Elliott, Hammer & Scholl, 1989). If young children are at risk for having hearing problems and thus learning problems, we should create an acoustic environment—especially in the early years—that would enable them to receive intelligible speech consistently and clearly.

2. Children with unilateral hearing impairments (hearing loss in only one ear) also will benefit from a soundfield system.

3. Children with slight permanent hearing impairments (15–25 dB hearing loss) might benefit more from a soundfield system than from a hearing aid in a classroom environment.

4. Children who have normal peripheral hearing sensitivity, but who are in special education classrooms due to language, learning, attending, or behavioral problems, would benefit from the increased instructional redundancy provided by a soundfield system. As many as three-fourths of the children in primary-level special education classrooms do not have normal hearing sensitivity, and their hearing problems usually have not been identified nor managed by the school systems (Flexer, 1989; Flexer, Millin, & Brown, 1990; Ray, Sarff, & Glassford, 1984).

5. Children with mild to moderate hearing impairments who wear hearing aids might do as well with a soundfield system as they would with a personal FM unit.

6. Children who have normal peripheral hearing sensitivity but who have difficulty processing, understanding, or attending to classroom instruction could benefit from soundfield technology.

7. Children for whom English is a second language benefit from a more intelligible signal provided by the enhanced S/N ratio of a soundfield system (Crandell, 1996). When one is learning a new language, how much of the acoustic signal needs to be heard to differentiate the new words of the language? All of the signal, every sound, every syllable, every word marker—the entire message needs to be intelligible because the child's brain is missing an internal program that would enable the child to fill in the blanks.

8. Children with cochlear implants also need an improved S/N ratio to receive intelligible speech. Soundfield technology provides a sufficient S/N ratio for many of these children.

With more and more schools incorporating principles of inclusion, where children who would have been in self-contained placements are in the mainstream classroom, soundfield systems offer a way of enhancing the classroom learning environment for the benefit of *all* children.

What's at stake in the development of early learning success is the creation of a new workforce for the new millennium. As our society becomes more technology-based, there is a great need for a highly literate work force. Currently, workers must read at least at a 9th-grade level to have access to job-related print materials. We must educate students who are capable of lifelong, flexible learning because people now change jobs or careers four to eight times during their work life. Enhancing the listening environment, therefore, is a critical task that can create the neurological foundations for learning success throughout the life span.

RESOURCES

Teachers and parents should consult with their school-based educational audiologist or with an audiologist in the community. An audiologist is an individual who holds a graduate degree and a state license for the diagnosis and treatment of hearing and hearing problems.

A 22-minute videotape made by Carol Flexer covers many of the issues addressed in this article. The tape is titled "Enhancing Classrooms for Listening, Language and Literacy" and can be purchased from INFO-LINK Video Bulletin, Box 852, Layton, Utah 84041; telephone: 801-544-1388; Web site: www.infolnks.com.

The following books provide additional information about soundfield amplification and present effective ways to work with children to expand their auditory capabilities:

Berg, F.S. (1993). *Acoustics and sound systems in schools,* San Diego: Singular Publishing Group.

Crandell, C. C., Smaldino, J. J., & Flexer, C. (1995). *Soundfield FM amplification: Theory and practical applications.* San Diego: Singular Publishing Group.

Flexer, C. (1999). *Facilitating hearing and listening in young children* (2nd ed.). San Diego: Singular Publishing Group.

Robertson, L. (2000). *Literacy learning for children who are deaf or hard of hearing.* Washington, DC: The Alexander Graham Bell Association for the Deaf and Hard of Hearing.

REFERENCES

American Speech-Language-Hearing Association. (March 1995). Position statement and guidelines for acoustics in educational settings. *American Speech-Language-Hearing Association, 37*(14), 15–19.

Berg, F. S. (1987). *Facilitating classroom listening: A handbook for teachers of normal and hard of hearing students.* Boston: College-Hill Press/Little Brown.

Berg, F. S. (1993). *Acoustics and sound systems in schools.* San Diego, CA: Singular Publishing Group.

Boothroyd, A. (1997). Auditory development of the hearing child. *Scandinavian Audiology, 26*(46), 9–16.

Chermak, G. D., & Musiek, F. E. (1997). *Central auditory processing disorders: New perspectives.* San Diego, CA: Singular Publishing Group.

Crandell, C. (1996). Effects of soundfield FM amplification on the speech perception of ESL children. *Educational Audiology Monograph, 4,* 1–5.

Crandell, C., & Smaldino, J. (1994). An update of classroom acoustics for children with hearing impairment. *The Volta Review, 96,* 291–306.

Crandell, C., Smaldino, J., & Flexer, C. (1995). *Soundfield FM amplification: Theory and practical applications.* San Diego, CA: Singular Publishing Group.

Elliott, L. L., Hammer, M. A., & Scholl, M. E. (1989). Fine grained auditory discrimination in normal children and children with language-learning problems. *Journal of Speech and Hearing Research, 32,* 112–119.

Flexer, C. (1989). Turn on sound: An odyssey of soundfield amplification. *Educational Audiology Association Newsletter, 5,* 6–7.

Flexer, C. (1999). *Facilitating hearing and listening in young children* (2nd ed.). San Diego, CA: Singular Publishing Group.

Flexer, C., Millin, J. P., & Brown, L. (1990). Children with developmental disabilities: The effect of soundfield amplification on word identification. *Language, Speech and Hearing Services in Schools, 21,* 177–182.

Flexer, C., Richards, C., Buie, C., & Brandy, W. (1994). Making the grade with amplification in classrooms. *Hearing Instruments, 45,* 24–26.

Gilbertson, M., & Bramlett, R. K. (1998). Phonological awareness screening to identify at-risk readers: Implications for practitioners. *Language, Speech and Hearing Services in Schools, 29,* 109–116.

Musiek, F. E., & Berge, B. E. (1998). A neuroscience view of auditory training/stimulation and central auditory processing disorders. In M. G. Masters, N. A. Stecker, & J. Katz (Eds.), *Central auditory processing disorders: Mostly management* (pp. 15–32). Boston: Allyn and Bacon.

Niskar, A. S., Kieszak, S. M., Holmes, A., Esteban, E., Rubin, C., & Brody, D. J. (1998). Prevalence of hearing loss among children 6 to 19 years: The Third National Health and Nutrition Examination Survey. *Journal of the American Medical Association, 279,* 1071–1075.

Ray, H., Sarff, L. S., & Glassford, F. E. (1984, Summer/Fall). Soundfield amplification: An innovative educational intervention for mainstreamed learning disabled students. *The Directive Teacher, 6*(1), 18–20.

Robertson, L. (2000). *Literacy learning for children who are deaf or hard of hearing.* Washington, DC: The Alexander Graham Bell Association for the Deaf and Hard of Hearing.

Instructional Support Teams: It's a Group Thing

James A. Tucker

A well-worn cliche asserts that *all* students should be successful in school. But having that statement as part of the school's mission statement and realizing it as an outcome are quite different things. For every student to be successful, there must be a basic plan that accommodates the specific learning needs of each student, one that doesn't discount the needs of some to the benefit of others. One of the emerging ideas that holds significant promise to accomplish such an objective is the concept of instructional support.

Instructional support is simply the most recent name of the concept. The initial flurry of reports has resulted from implementation of the concept in Pennsylvania (Kovaleski, Tucker, & Duffy, 1995; Kovaleski, Tucker, & Stevens, 1996; Kovaleski, Gickling, Morrow, & Swank, 1999), but the concept really has its roots in Connecticut, where it has been implemented under the name "Early Intervention Project" (EIP) since 1985 (Connecticut State Department of Education, 1994).

By introducing a simple collection of proven educational practices under the rubric of instructional support, schools in at least four states have systematically and significantly reduced the number of referrals to special education while at the same time seeing an increase in academic achievement and a decrease in grade retention. And according to a comprehensive study by Hartman and Fay (1996), this has been accomplished with no increase in cost to the district over a 5- to 10-year period.

What follows is a brief description of the principles or elements of the instructional support concept, a brief rationale to support the selection of these elements, and a concluding section that provides examples of data that support the validity of the concept.

WHAT DOES INSTRUCTIONAL SUPPORT LOOK LIKE?

Instructional support is a concept, not a model. A model has formal structure and a specific pattern to be followed, whereas a concept implies a set of basic principles. The implementation of such a concept in any given location may cause it to look and sound different from other applications of the same concept implemented elsewhere. But there are common aspects of all successful applications of this concept, and this chapter will identify and support those common characteristics.

The fundamental elements of the instructional support concept are as follows:

1. Problems with individual students are usually good indicators of more fundamental problems in the system. See "The 85/15 Rule" (Scholtes, Joiner, & Streibel, 1996), which holds that 85 percent of all problems in an organization are systems concerns and only 15 percent are fundamentally individual person (student) problems.

2. The units of measure for reporting and evaluating results are the individual child, the classroom, and the individual school building (site). It is the aggregation of these units of measure that provides meaningful system (school district) measures.

3. The school building administrator is in charge of all aspects of the program in his or her building. This responsibility includes monitoring the quality of instruction and being aware of what effective instruction is and how it should be assessed. Effective leadership on the part of the building administrator is key to realizing success for all students.

4. Individual student referrals at the school building site are primarily requests for assistance in the regular classroom. They should be viewed as a system opportunity, rather than possible irritants to be removed from the regular classroom.

5. There is a dynamic team at the building site to which teachers can go for assistance.

6. At least one instructional support professional is an integral member of the team. This professional is a highly trained, experienced teacher with

no regular classroom or class load, whose time is dedicated to such instructional support activities as collaborative consultation with instructional personnel and in-classroom demonstration of effective instructional strategies. Generally schools have one such person for every 500 students at the elementary/middle school level.

7. Highly specific and skill-oriented training is provided at the school building level in the following areas:

a. Collaborative consultation. (See Rosenfield & Gravois, 1996.)

b. Instructional assessment. (See Gickling & Rosenfield, 1995; Tucker, 1985.)

c. Behavior management. (See Valentine, 1987.)

d. Curriculum adaptation. (See Huck, Myers, & Wilson, 1989)

8. The form of the training is programmed to maximize the results expected with students in the regular classroom. General aspects of the training are as follows:

a. Most of the training is "hands-on" in classrooms via guided practice.

b. Differentiated training is provided for the building administrator, the instructional support professional, and all the teachers in the building.

c. Intensive site-based training lasts for at least one full year; followup site-based training continues for at least three more years—probably an additional five to 10 years.

d. The trainers must be experienced in the skills involved and provide most of the training by guided practice in classrooms—*not* in didactic workshops (though some such training is also involved). This is not a model where the trainers can attend a trainer-of-trainers seminar or get a book and "bone up" on the method and then provide training.

The instructional support concept is built on three basic foundation ideas, each of which will be discussed briefly:

1. Support by a team of caring and trained professionals—the instructional support team.

2. Application of the factors that characterize effective schools.

3. Focus on effective instruction.

THE INSTRUCTIONAL SUPPORT TEAM: AN APPLICATION OF COOPERATIVE LEARNING

Instructional support is an application of collaborative learning in the search for more effective instructional strategies. Just as cooperative learning is a powerful tool in the classroom, so is instructional support a powerful tool within a school. Solving the problems presented by student learners is a learning process just as surely as is an assignment in school. And the same process that works in the classroom works in the solution of the problems that are presented for consideration in the instructional support process.

Using Kagan's (1994) description of cooperative learning, for example, there are three basic principles: Simultaneous Interaction, Positive Interdependence, and Individual Accountability. What happens when these principles are applied to the function of instructional support teams? Actually, something quite dramatic occurs, but only when two more dimensions are addressed: leadership and effective instruction.

EFFECTIVE SCHOOLS

Even at its best, the instructional support concept is only an interim tool to help us get to the ideal, which is nicely presented by the effective schools literature. Arthur Steller (1988) makes the following statement about the effective schools research findings:

> . Although there are variations in the school effectiveness research, five factors seem to be consistent across studies. These are:
> 1. Strong instructional leadership by the principal.
> 2. Clear instructional focus.
> 3. High expectations and standards.
> 4. Safe and orderly climate.
> 5. Frequent monitoring of student achievement.
> Apparently these factors interact with one another to produce a good school (Gage, 1978). All must coexist for significant positive results to occur.

Assuming that these five factors of school effectiveness are real and that success for all students is facilitated by their presence, it is important to make sure that any systematic program application includes all five of them.

Instructional support, as a concept, could be described as a way of implementing what was shown by the effective schools research, but with a specific focus on effective instruction in the regular classroom.

A FOCUS ON EFFECTIVE INSTRUCTION

In the early 1980s, the state of Connecticut was faced with a challenge: There was a significant disproportion of minority students in special education classes. The state decided to do something about it, but what? Fortunately, there appeared a publication (Heller, Holtzman, & Messick, 1982) that set forth the new finding that such discrimination was not due, as had been thought, to biased testing, but rather to inefficient referral systems based on ineffective instruction. This conclusion was supported soon thereafter by Samuels (1984), who addressed specifically what should be done to provide all students with a foundation of basic skills (reading, writing, mathematics, speaking, and listening).

In 1984, the National School Psychology Inservice Training Network published *School Psychology: The State of the Art*, in which a different paradigm began to emerge to meet the needs of students who were not being successful in school (Ysseldyke, 1984). In that publication, a model for instructional intervention was provided by Samuels (1984). It is a simple statement, but it had profound results that have now extended to thousands of schools in many states:

> In many ways, good athletic coaching and good classroom teaching have much in common, and principles of coaching applied to the classroom can help students master the basic skills.
> In essence, to master the basic skills either in sports or the classroom, three elements are necessary:
> 1. Motivate the student.
> 2. Bring the student to the level of accuracy in the skill.
> 3. Provide the practice necessary for the skill to become automatic.

While subsequently there appeared a number of useful and perhaps more comprehensive frameworks to describe the instructional process, it was this conceptual framework of instructional success, provided by Samuels, that guided the development and implementation of instructional support from the mid-1980s to the present.

In Pennsylvania, the instructional support concept was implemented as a statewide reform of the interaction between special education and regular education. Instructional support became the first form of intervention when a student was experiencing academic difficulty. Subsequent referral or more intensive programming was provided if needed, but with the added benefit of the data derived from the instructional support.

In the application of instructional support that was implemented in Pennsylvania, the frame of reference begins with a student's identified need—not with an identified or suspected disability. Once a student's need is determined, the services or programs needed to meet that need are based on the nature of the need, not on what services or programs are available or can be conveniently provided. Finally, the delivery of all services is managed at the school building level, under the direction of the building administrator or the administrator's designee, not at the district or regional level. "The most significant change in the regulations was to focus on instructional needs of students, rather than on perceived internal deficiencies of students. . . . The new regulations require that referral for special education evaluation be *preceded* by interventions of an instructional support team (IST)" (Feir, 1995).

HOW DOES INSTRUCTIONAL SUPPORT WORK ON A DAY-TO-DAY BASIS?

Because instructional support is a concept, it is implemented in many ways. What follows is a somewhat eclectic description of how instructional support is carried out at a school building level. The reader should keep in mind that this is simply the most common representation of how the concept is put into place.

Instructional support involves two primary forms of action: the action of the IST and the action of the teacher assigned to provide the instructional support.

THE INSTRUCTIONAL SUPPORT CONSULTANT

The primary action on a day-to-day basis is performed by the instructional support consultant (ISC). Remember that this consultant is a teacher who has been trained in instructional support strategies, which are conducted for one student, a small group of students, or an entire class in the regular classroom. The assigned task on any given day may come from the IST, from a request log, or by verbal request.

Typically, there is some kind of a log book or recording sheet in the building administrator's office on which teachers throughout the building are invited to place their names along with brief descriptions of the issues they would like to have addressed in their classrooms. The issue may be a concern for an individual student, but it may also be a request for a demonstration of an instructional strategy that will be used with the whole class. For some ISCs, the referrals come even more informally from a teacher or the building administrator simply asking for assistance, but it is always better to have a record of the requested action. A record is especially needed at the point that the IST comes into play. But it is important to keep the necessary recording to a minimum at this stage. There should be no referral form or other complicated formal procedure to obtain the help of the ISC. A simple request log maintained in the building administrator's office is usually sufficient.

The ISC, in consultation with the building administrator, establishes the priority of issues to be addressed. And the ISC proceeds to spend the day accordingly, dealing with specific cases in regular classrooms. This is not a pull-out service, though that should not be read as disallowing one-on-one support wherever it is most advantageous. Normally it is a service provided in the regular classroom setting. And even students in regular classrooms sometimes receive instruction outside that setting (e.g., trumpet lessons are probably never provided in the regular classroom). The principle here is that the location of the instructional support should be determined by the nature of the support, not by some eligibility factor.

What the ISC does in the classroom is dictated by the needs of the individual student or teacher. The action may be an instructional assessment of a student's reading fluency or comprehension, leading to specific interventions based on that student's prior knowledge in order to maximize achievement. It may also be a classwide intervention to model or demonstrate a given strategy that will benefit not only one or two students, but the entire class. Learning these skills and becoming skilled in them is a major portion of the training that is provided in the implementation of instructional support.

At the end of each day, the ISC usually records the day's activities in terms of results, observations, needs for additional help or consultation, and so forth. Further, the ISC should accumulate those daily records into an aggregation of data over time.

THE INSTRUCTIONAL SUPPORT TEAM (IST)

The IST is the basic support group for the ISC as well as for all the educators in the building. There are many versions of the instructional support team. An excellent resource for developing functional ISTs is the book by Rosenfield and Gravois (1996). They call this team an "instructional consultation team" and describe its function as "to serve as a centralized problem-solving unit, to model interactive professionalism (Fullan & Hargreaves, 1991), and to operate as a consultant panel for each other and for teachers in the building" (p. 40).

The IST is a group of colleagues who will both model collaboration and provide expertise as needed. They may meet on a regular schedule or on an as-needed basis.

The membership of the IST also varies from place to place. Membership may represent various programs, or it may be an appointed group, with permanent membership supplemented by individuals with specific expertise as needed. The team may be as small as the building administrator, the ISC, and the teacher who is making a request.

When putting such a team structure into place, the vital role of parents must be included in the process of collaboration and problem solving that is facilitated by such a team. Parental involvement on the IST is critical to success for all students.

Each team should be built around the culture of the school building and made as formal or informal as is appropriate for a team in that setting.

TWO DAYS IN THE LIFE
OF AN INSTRUCTIONAL SUPPORT CONSULTANT

What follows are excerpts from the personal journal entries of an instructional support consultant over two days of service.

Tuesday

What a day! I am thoroughly exhausted. We got home from school at 8:30 PM. . . .

. . . I taught a paragraph model to the 7th-graders last week. Today, they were all ready to write their paragraphs. It was the best and most incredible writing lesson I have ever seen. Every single student was completely engaged and they were excited about their accomplishments. The 30 or so students who are failing and "just won't do anything" were so incredibly on task and they flew through their paragraphs. . . . I reached 113 students today with an IST intervention. That was so much more than I could have done working with one student at a time in a pull-out situation.

After school I taught 3 hours of Kagan Cooperative Learning, Session 1 (Kagan, 1994) and then stayed for 7th-grade juggling night. A great day, but a tiring one.

Thursday

I am already seeing some incredible results from my work in the classrooms. The 7th-graders are doing so much better because of the strategies that I used with them in English class. They are all pleased with themselves because they have written such developed paragraphs, and "it was easy!" The structure I added helped all of the students. Several of the "targeted IST" students are suddenly doing really well in English and are just beaming with pride. Now, they are motivated to start getting their work done for their other classes so they can be passing them as well. One student in particular stands out. Everyone had written him off as a big "failure." He couldn't be happier now. He was creating a slide show today for the book he is reading for English. Another teacher happened to walk in and see him so intently engaged and was amazed! I said magic is not going to happen, but that was "magic!" Obviously, it didn't just happen by itself.

. . . I intend to keep going. I am working with the social studies teacher next week. I am going to teach a note-taking strategy on Mon. and Tues. The teacher is reviewing on Wed. and testing on Thurs. Most of the students I talk with say they don't study and that they don't know how to study. Many students told me today that they would like to know how. So, I asked the social studies teacher if I could teach the students a strategy or two on Wed. to use when studying for their tests.

What a difference I am able to make by integrating into the classroom instead of working with a few students at a time on a pull-out basis!

I am also sharing the successes I am seeing at each team meeting. My office mate suggested I carry student work with me and show it off whenever I have an audience. So, I am armed and ready.

The two teachers from the elementary building who observed me on Tuesday have spread to several other teachers about how incredible it was that all of the students were engaged.

One more exciting thought. I was talking with the technology coordinator (my office mate) about all of this, and at one point in the conversation he said, "It sounds like you are making a difference with one student at a time." . . . That is the underlying motto of IST. I was sharing this with William, and he said that is what the letters IST stand for: I (one) S(student) at a T(time). I can't wait to create a visual of this to share with the teams. The problem I see is that everyone feels so overwhelmed by the thought of "fixing" the large numbers of students who need help. They don't think they have the time, energy, etc., so avoid trying. The beauty of IST is that we don't have to tackle the entire population at once. We just start with one student. This takes the pressure off and makes it seem achievable. . . . This success spreads quickly and fosters motivation on everyone's part. It is the same with teachers. One teacher has success with a new strategy and shares that success in passing with another teacher.

Results from Instructional Support Teams

As with any innovation, the proof of the program is in the results, not in the eloquence and persuasive nature of the concepts involved. The reader is encouraged to review all of the references provided and to contact persons in the states of Connecticut, Pennsylvania, New York, and Michigan where the instructional support concept has been in operation for long enough to show the kinds of results shared below.

Reduction in Special Education Referrals

During the 1990–91 academic year, ISTs were implemented in 186 schools (individual school building sites) in 104 school districts throughout the state of Pennsylvania. During that year, there was an average reduction of 45 percent in special education placement in those buildings. At the same time, there was a reduction of 15 percent in regular education grade retention. The measure of retention was used as one way of determining whether the issues requiring intervention were being ignored and therefore contributing to student retention as opposed to placement in special education. For a comprehensive report on this connection, see Kovaleski et al. (1996).

Beginning with the 1985–86 academic year, the instructional support concept was implemented in individual school buildings in eight school districts in Connecticut. As an example of the results, Figure 6.1 shows the special education placement rate at one of the school building sites before and after the introduction of instructional support. The most remarkable fact illustrated by these data is the consistency over time that has resulted from the initial years of training. What is shown is a systems change at the building level.

It is worth noting that the school site illustrated in Figure 6.1 is an inner-city school where 70 percent of the students are Hispanic and African American. As stated earlier in the chapter, there was concern in Connecticut as to the over-representation of minority students in special education. During the first four years of implementation, data were collected relative to the special-education placement of minority students.

Figure 6.2 shows that the proportion of minority placements into special education was substantially reduced after the introduction of instructional support, and it continued to remain at more equalized levels over the subsequent years for which data were collected. Before the introduction of instructional support, the percentage of referred students who were placed

FIGURE 6.1

SPECIAL EDUCATION PLACEMENT HISTORY

BEFORE AND AFTER INTRODUCTION OF INSTRUCTIONAL SUPPORT (IS)

Academic Year	Total Enrollment	Placements Into Special Ed.	
1984–85 (Pre-IS)	675	53	(8%)
1985–86	682	14	(2%)
1986–87	705	14	(2%)
1987–88	716	13	(2%)
1988–89	727	18	(2%)
1989–90	809	7	(1%)
1990–91	819	10	(1%)
1991–92	792	13	(2%)
1992–93	689	13	(2%)
1993–94	678	16	(2%)
1994–95	711	13	(2%)
1995–96	678	16	(2%)
1996–97	580	9	(2%)
1997–98	591	6	(1%)

into special education were 95 percent for Hispanic students, 36 percent for African American students, and 48 percent for Caucasian students. After four years of instructional support, these percentages were 7 percent for Hispanic students, 3 percent for African American students, and 3 percent for Caucasian students. Those who previously would have been referred, evaluated, and placed were now getting instructional support in their regular classrooms and no longer needed special education services.

INCREASE IN ACADEMIC ACHIEVEMENT

Perhaps the most impressive outcome of instructional support is the fact that student achievement has improved. Students who were struggling aren't any more; students who were not reading are now; students whose misbehavior was the result of boredom or frustration are declared by their teachers to be behaving. Why is it so easy to overlook the fact that these results are what school is all about?

FIGURE 6.2

SPECIAL EDUCATION PLACEMENT RATES BY ETHNIC/RACIAL PROPORTION BEFORE AND AFTER INTRODUCTION OF INSTRUCTIONAL SUPPORT (IS)

School Year	Referred	Placed	Percent
Hispanic			
1984–85 (Pre-IS)	40	38	95%
1985–86	33	8	24%
1986–87	96	7	7%
1987–88	87	7	8%
1988–89	96	7	7%
African American			
1984–85 (Pre-IS)	11	4	36%
1985–86	6	2	33%
1986–87	15	1	7%
1987–88	15	0	0%
1988–89	29	1	3%
Caucasian			
1984–85 (Pre-IS)	21	10	48%
1985–86	23	3	13%
1986–87	43	9	21%
1987–88	34	6	18%
1988–89	30	1	3%

The data exist in two forms: instructional assessment data (e.g., Kovaleski et al., 1999) and standardized test scores. Both forms of data show consistent and positive increases when IS is used. The accumulation of these data will be reported elsewhere, but one example will provide the kind of results most often reported. Figure 6.3 shows the one-year increase in reading achievement after introduction of instructional support for 16 6th-grade students from a special-education resource room. This classroom was in a medium-size town in an otherwise rural part of an eastern state, which suffered serious economic slowdown with the collapse of the steel industry in the United States.

To achieve these results, this resource room class of 16 students was taught as a regular class, using cooperative learning groups and the curriculum of general education, adapted to fit the prior knowledge of each student in the class.

FIGURE 6.3

READING COMPREHENSION BEFORE AND AFTER INTRODUCTION OF INSTRUCTIONAL SUPPORT (IS)

Student	Reading Vocabulary		Reading Comprehension	
	Fall (Pre-IS)	Spring (Post-IS)	Fall (Pre-IS)	Spring (Post-IS)
Student 1	2.4	5.1	2.6	4.7
Student 2	3.7	8.5	3.6	5.5
Student 3	4.4	5.6	3.0	4.5
Student 4	5.1	10.1	6.8	7.9
Student 5	6.0	11.2	5.5	12.4
Student 6	4.7	9.1	2.8	5.8
Student 7	3.0	5.1	3.0	3.6
Student 8	3.0	5.4	2.7	2.9
Student 9	3.5	7.1	3.1	4.7
Student 10	3.5	6.0	3.8	6.8
Student 11	4.4	9.1	4.1	5.1
Student 12	2.1	3.5	3.5	4.1
Student 13	3.3	5.6	4.1	5.4
Student 14	3.0	7.1	4.1	4.9
Student 15	2.9	5.1	4.1	3.8
Student 16	3.3	7.1	3.6	4.9
Averages	3.6	6.8	3.8	5.4
Gains	+ 3.2/student		+1.5/student	

Note: Reading comprehension is measured by the Stanford Achievement Test.

REDUCTION IN GRADE RETENTION

Kovaleski et al. (1995) report the effect on grade retention of the introduction of instructional support in Pennsylvania. They report data to show that during the initial three-year period of providing instructional support, 99 individual school buildings demonstrated a 67 percent reduction in grade retention. It is important to note that this improvement was accomplished with a simultaneous 33- to 46-percent reduction in special education placement.

COST-EFFECTIVENESS

A comprehensive evaluation of the cost-effectiveness of the IST concept in Pennsylvania was performed by the Center for Special Educational Finance (Hartman & Fay, 1996):

> In summary, the effectiveness of the IST program was much greater than the traditional program; it was able to reduce the number of students placed in special education, while at the same time providing extensive and successful instructional services to many more children in regular education. It did this at a cost that was no greater than the traditional program over a 5- to 10-year period (p. 32).

IMPORTANT CAVEAT

There are many innovative models and concepts being proposed in the literature, and there are many more that have come and gone over the past several decades. What makes us comfortable in supporting and promoting the concept of instructional support are the results that have been observed in a wide variety of locations and under varying conditions. It is important that any such concept be subjected to rigorous evaluation before adoption. I am particularly impressed by the evaluation model provided by Ellis and Fouts (1997). They propose that any innovation being considered for adoption pass three levels of research validation: a sound theoretical base, valid classroom application, and consistent "evidence of large-scale implementation" (p. 249).

Relative to the third level of validation, a difficult aspect has always been to implement the innovation in a form consistent with the principles on which it is based. For example, when teachers say they are doing cooperative learning in their classrooms, are they fulfilling all the necessary ingredients of cooperative learning, or are they simply assigning tasks to a group of students? Group work is not, by itself, cooperative learning.

Kovaleski et al. (1999) report specifically on the results of high versus low implementation of instructional support teams in Pennsylvania. The data in this study clearly show that to obtain positive results in achievement, there had to be high implementation of the concept. The schools were rank-ordered in terms of the degree to which they were implementing *all* the elements of instructional support. High implementation schools were defined as those in the top 30 percent of the ranking. The authors of the study make the following statement in conclusion:

What is striking about these results is the implication that half-hearted efforts at IST implementation are not better for at-risk students than what is traditionally practiced in non-IST schools. In examining these findings, we are reminded that "educational insanity" refers to doing the same thing over and over again, but expecting different results. Such results occur all too often in education when schools adopt new initiatives in name only, without fidelity to essential program design features. In evaluating the IST process, it was essential to examine the different treatment effects based on how faithfully individual schools implemented the IST initiative. Without this type of compelling data, it would have been impossible to account for the effectiveness of the IST process. Given the scope of the study and the size of the data pool, the results are generalizable and reaffirm the importance of maintaining the fidelity of the IST process (p. 180).

CONCLUSION

The concept of instructional support is not new, of course. It is the application of principles of effective instruction that have been present for a long time. In 1682, William Penn wrote the following statute into the *Fundamental Laws of the Province of Pennsylvania*:

All persons having children shall cause such to be instructed in reading and writing, so that they may be able to read the scriptures and to write by the time they attain to twelve years of age and that then they be taught some useful trade or skill.

Setting aside the fact that the fundamental basal reader was the Bible and that mathematics was taught as a job skill, contained within this early American mandate are three fundamental principles of education: Parents are the responsible agents; basic skills are the foundation of the curriculum; and the expected outcome is preparation for a functional adult life.

Some 300 years later, current research has certainly re-established the pragmatic truth of these time-honored concepts. Instructional support teams provide a mechanism through which collaborative adult problem solving is used to help every student develop the basic skills necessary for success in life.

REFERENCES

Connecticut State Department of Education. (1994). *The Early Intervention Project.* Middletown, CT: Special Education Resource Center, Connecticut State Department of Education.

Ellis, A., & Fouts, J. (1997). *Research on Educational Innovations* (2nd ed.). Princeton Junction, NJ: Eye on Education Publishers.

Feir, R. E. (1995, March). *Refining Pennsylvania's funding mechanism and program rules for special education.* Paper presented at the annual meeting of the American Education Finance Association, New Orleans.

Fullan, M., & Hargreaves. A. (1991). *What's worth fighting for? Working together for your school.* Andover, MA: Regional Laboratory for Educational Improvement of the Northeast and Islands.

Gage, N. (1978). *The scientific basis of the art of teaching.* New York: Teachers College Press.

Gickling, E. E., & Rosenfield, S. (1995). Curriculum-based assessment. In A. Thomas & J. Grimes (Eds.), *Best practices in school psychology* (pp. 587–595). Washington, DC: National Association of School Psychologists.

Hartman, W. T., & Fay, T. A. (1996). *Cost-effectiveness of instructional support teams in Pennsylvania.* Policy Paper No. 9 of the Center for Special Education Finance. Palo Alto, CA: American Institutes for Research.

Heller, K. A., Holtzman, W. H., & Messick, S. (Eds.). (1982). *Placing children in special education: A strategy for equity.* Washington, DC: National Academy Press.

Huck, R., Myers, R., & Wilson, J. (1989). *ADAPT: A developmental activity program for teachers* (2nd ed.). Pittsburgh, PA: Allegheny Intermediate Unit.

Kagan, S. (1994). *Cooperative learning.* San Juan Capistrano, CA: Kagan Cooperative Learning.

Kovaleski, J. F., Gickling, E. E., Morrow, H., & Swank, P. R. (1999). High versus low implementation of instructional support teams: A case for maintaining program fidelity. *Remedial and Special Education, 20*(3), 170–183.

Kovaleski, J. F., Tucker, J. A., & Duffy, D. J., Jr. (1995). School reform through instructional support: The Pennsylvania initiative, Part I. *Communique,* published by the National Association of School Psychologists, *23*(8), insert.

Kovaleski, J. F., Tucker, J. A., & Stevens, L. J. (1996). Bridging special and regular education: The Pennsylvania initiative. *Educational Leadership, 53*(5), 44–47.

Penn, W. (1682). *Fundamental Laws of the Province of Pennsylvania.*

Rosenfield, S. A., & Gravois, T. (1996). *Instructional Consultation Teams.* New York: The Guilford Press.

Samuels, J. (1984). Basic academic skills. In J. E. Ysseldyke, *School psychology: The state of the art.* Minneapolis: National School Psychology Inservice Training Network, University of Minnesota.

Scholtes, P. R., Joiner, B. L., & Streibel, B. J. (1996). *The Team Handbook* (3rd ed.). Madison, WI: Oriel Inc.

Steller, A. W. (1988). *Effective schools research: Practice and promise.* Bloomington, IN: Phi Delta Kappa Educational Foundation.

Tucker, J. A. (1985). Curriculum-based assessment: An introduction. *Exceptional Children 52*(3), 199–204.

Valentine, M. (1987). *How to deal with discipline problems in the schools: A practical guide for educators.* Dubuque, IA: Kendall/Hunt.

Ysseldyke, J. (1984). *School psychology: The state of the art.* Minneapolis: National School Psychology Inservice Training Network, University of Minnesota.

THE INSTRUCTIONAL SUPPORT TEAM CONCEPT IN ACTION

Kenneth F. Pawlowski

If educators truly believe that all students can learn, special attention must be given to differentiating instruction. Any such commitment must take into account the accommodation of a variety of learning styles as well as a sensitivity to varying degrees of learning readiness. Focusing on individual learning styles and identifying appropriate teaching strategies to address them is at the core of the instructional support team (IST) concept being implemented at Silver Springs Elementary School in Northville, Michigan. Classroom teachers work closely with a team of specialists to analyze learning difficulties and brainstorm appropriate interventions. The process empowers classroom teachers to take responsibility for the learning of *all* their students. Support is given so that emotional, behavioral, and academic needs of students are met in the regular classroom setting. As a result of this process, special education referrals and placements have been reduced, and reallocation of resources has been possible.

Classroom teachers traditionally have been sensitive to students who are experiencing learning difficulties. But dealing with those difficulties in the regular classroom has been challenging and, in some cases, frustrating. Factors such as large class size and lack of time hampered classroom teachers as they attempted to reteach various skills. Student progress was characterized as too slow or nonexistent. Thus, suspecting a learning disability and providing additional support became an appealing alternative. Special education placements were made, all too often, based on the belief that necessary individual attention was more likely to take place with the involvement of special education staff typically in an exclusive environment. The IST concept has reduced classroom teacher frustration by having specialists available to immediately supply needed services in the regular classroom. These additional services included team teaching, individual pullout, small-group instruction, visual memory training, motor development activities, and in-service opportunities. These strategies are employed with delayed learners at Silver Springs. Our goal is to address effectively the needs of a variety of learning styles.

THE BELIEFS OF THE INSTRUCTIONAL SUPPORT TEAM

Essential in the development and implementation of such a support system is the necessity for staff to develop and commit to certain beliefs. After a great deal of soul searching and discussion, the staff at Silver Springs Elementary School formalized our beliefs as follows:

We believe:
- in reducing the amount of time a student flounders before appropriate intervention is provided.
- that the most effective learning occurs in the regular classroom.
- that effective intervention must include the identification of individual learning styles.
- that the most powerful interventions are developed collaboratively.
- that teachers will accept responsibility and ownership for student learning when appropriate support is provided.

The articulation of these belief statements spurred special education leaders on the staff and the administration to approach the staff for support. Support was secured incrementally over a four-year period. Year 1 focused on getting the staff to recognize the need for the process, developing the instructional support framework, and sharing that process with staff. Year 2 involved formally establishing the position of the instructional support teacher and integrating the process with the school improvement plan. Year 3 involved making modifications to the process as a result of feedback from teachers. Year 4 focused on developing a recording system that allowed staff to chart the use of implemented strategies and their success relative to the student involved. By the end of Year 4, an intervention process was in place, which focused on providing the classroom teacher with the knowledge and skills necessary to confidently deal with the different rates of learning in the classroom.

THE INTERVENTION PROCESS

The established intervention process features the following three steps:

• Peer conferencing, which allows the classroom teacher to document and inform parents of the concern, review student files for additional information, seek assistance from colleagues, and implement suggestions made.

• Instructional support intervention requires that the teacher's concern be articulated and written in observable terms. A meeting is held with appropriate staff, and a plan is developed which identifies specific strategies and interventions to improve the student's achievement in the given area. Time frames are established at this point. This phase of the process continues until the teacher verifies that the student is making appreciable progress, or until lack of progress warrants special education testing.

• Comprehensive team intervention (child study) stage, which allows for convening meetings of a traditional individual educational planning team. Special education forms are completed by appropriate staff and recommended testing is conducted as per parent permission. If special education testing is not appropriate, adaptation plans are developed by the Instructional Support Team (school psychologist, instructional support teacher, resource room teacher, school social worker, language arts specialist, and principal). Formal statements as to a student's status are documented, along with a plan to monitor and adjust if necessary.

THE INSTRUCTIONAL SUPPORT TEAM'S IMPACT

The IST concept has had a positive effect on the general school climate. With differentiated instruction, all students have experienced a certain level of success; they feel supported and more willing to take risks as they learn. Because they feel good about themselves, they feel good about their school and their teachers. Consequently, discipline referrals are down, and teachers report a high level of respect in their classrooms. Staff morale is high. Teachers feel empowered to help those students who require more practice, alternative methods of instruction, or more time. The feelings of hopelessness when dealing with students who "just don't get it" are minimized. With the help of various strategies and support staff, every student can experience a level of success. Classroom teachers openly accept the responsibility for educating all students in their classroom.

Parents respond positively when their children demonstrate progress. Dealing with confident teachers assures them that their child can learn. Seeing the "team approach" work with their child encourages them to be part of the process. They quickly realize that parents play a key role in the educational process. The trauma that special education placement can have on all involved is often avoided.

A successful IST concept requires that we capitalize on the desire of well-intentioned teachers to effectively teach all their students and that we quickly establish credible and supportive relationships with them. Being responsive to their colleagues allows IST members to set a course for success, a success that encompasses *all* children. IST has led directly to a reduction in our resource room teacher's caseload and in special education referrals. Consequently, focus has shifted to preventing early learning failure. At the same time, teachers are comfortable working collaboratively with IST team members in an effort to promote student success. The progress of our IST process is summarized in Figure 7.1.

Intervention strategies we used include developing a building-based instructional support team, motor-skill development programs, visual memory training, co-teaching in the early grades, and use of soundfield FM amplification systems.

FIGURE 7.1
SILVER SPRINGS ELEMENTARY SCHOOL INSTRUCTIONAL SUPPORT TEAM AND SPECIAL EDUCATION REFERRALS

School Year	School Population	Students Referred to IST	Students Referred to Special Ed.	Certified Special Education Caseload
1993–94	250	0	18	34
1994–95	308	0	17	29
1995–96	344	0	14	20
1996–97	355	20	4	13
1997–98	339	25	4	10
1998–99	384	29	4	6
1999–00	477	27	6	7

Even though the advantages of the IST concept seem obvious (students benefit by quickly receiving intervention; students are not prematurely "labeled" as special education; teachers learn new strategies that can be applied with many students), it should not be considered the answer for dealing with all youngsters who are experiencing delays in their learning. Special education supports and services will still be necessary for some children.

VISION AND LEARNING

Nancy Sornson

Suzanna is a beautiful, bright 6-year-old child who is struggling in kindergarten. She can't remember how the alphabet letters and numbers look, and she prints her name illegibly. She is clumsy and bumps into other children in line, although her classmates are tolerant because she is friendly and well liked. Coloring, puzzles, dot-to-dots, cutting, bead work, and other near-point visual tasks are difficult. Her teacher describes her as extremely active and easily distracted, especially when asked to do any sustained activity like drawing or journal work. She loves the playground, but her balance is poor, so she avoids climbing equipment and the raised balance beams and tire walk.

At first glance we might define Suzanna as hyperactive, immature, difficult, tuned-out, or learning disabled. A closer look reveals that Suzanna is delayed in her motor and visual skill development. She is struggling in class because her nearpoint visual skills are not ready to handle sustained table work. Her poor balance keeps her from sitting calmly and attending easily. She has not yet developed a clear sense of her body's position in space. She will need intervention quickly if she is going to be a successful learner. Otherwise, Suzanna will begin on a path of early learning failure from which she may never reach her potential.

Many young children fall behind in school largely because their visual systems do not work well. These visual problems may not show up on the yearly school vision test. School vision screenings are designed to test acuity—what a child sees clearly at near and far points. Vision is more than acuity, however; vision is a complex brain process requiring perception, understanding, and the following skills:

- **Acuity:** clearness of vision at far and near points.
- **Tracking and fixation:** the ability to point the eyes accurately at an object and keep the eyes on a target whether it is stationary or moving. Reading smoothly and quickly across a page is an example.
- **Accommodation:** the ability to adjust the focus of the eyes from far to near point. Copying from the chalkboard requires the eyes to shift from the desk to the board easily and accurately.
- **Convergence:** the ability of the eyes to turn inward or outward when looking at objects from near to far. These skills must closely coordinate with accommodation skills.
- **Binocular fusion:** the ability to coordinate and align the eyes precisely so that the brain can fuse the input it receives from each eye. A slight problem here can cause double vision, and the brain may react by suppressing the use of one eye.
- **Eye-hand coordination:** the ability of the brain to interpret and coordinate the information it gets from the eye to direct the hands. Printing, coloring, and cutting require the use of eye-hand coordination.
- **Visual form perception and memory:** the ability to recognize letters, organize them into words, and remember what they look like. This is a most important skill for beginning readers.

Neurobiologists tell us that much of our vision is developed in the first year of life. At birth babies have limited vision. Their pupils constrict in a well-lit room, and they can distinguish sharp outlines, such as large objects or people's faces at close range. At 3 months their eyes can follow mom or dad across a room. Convergence and beginning depth perception develop around 1 year of age and are confirmed when a child crawls to a staircase and stops instead of tumbling down. At approximately 18 months, visual form perception begins, and a child can recognize similar but unlike visual images in books, such as pictures of dogs, cats, moms, books, and bottles. By age 3 a child can identify visual symbols within his or her experience, such as the "M" for McDonald's. Eye-hand coordination develops slowly from birth as the child is given experiences handling and playing with objects and feeding himself. Children who have good health and lots of opportunity to move and explore will usually develop vision normally. By the time they reach kindergarten, they should have an excellent visual system ready to handle the introduction of large print such as alphabet letters and numbers.

WHAT INTERFERES
WITH NORMAL DEVELOPMENT?

Many things can interfere with this normal developmental process. Illness, head or eye injury, disease, high fever, and poor motor skill development can cause a significant visual problem. A professional eye exam in the early years is important, especially if a parent suspects a problem or has a family history of visual difficulty or disease. All children should have a comprehensive eye examination by an optometrist or an ophthalmologist before entering kindergarten. A comprehensive examination includes an evaluation to determine how a patient is using the whole visual system, including acuity, eye teaming, focusing, tracking, and higher-order visual skills such as visual-spatial awareness, visualization, and visual memory.

Perhaps the most significant and growing problem we face with five- and six-year-old students is lack of appropriate visual-motor stimulation and experience. Many children are not getting enough good physical activity. Children learn through movement and play, and they need time on the floor to move and explore as infants. They also need colorful objects to look at and feel. Unfortunately, some children spend their days in homes or day-care settings where movement is limited. Outdoor play is not a priority due to space, supervision, or safety concerns. Even indoor movement is discouraged by the use of playpens, high chairs, rolling walkers, swings, etc. We continue to limit movement by strapping our children in car seats. By the time a child is 3, he or she has spent 500–600 hours in a car seat, deprived of hours of learning through movement. Young children need to run, jump, throw, catch, kick, climb, hop, and swing to develop their motor systems and visual systems. Playing outdoors in a safe environment with natural light, varied topography, and interesting things to look at using both near and far vision is important during the early years of development.

Excessive use of television, video, and computer games slows children's visual development by limiting movement experiences, hand-eye interactions, and imaginative play, and by offering entrancing visual images that remove the need for children to make visual thoughts of their own.

WHAT HAPPENS WHEN
CHILDREN ENTER SCHOOL?

When children enter school with less than optimal visual systems, problems begin. Some problems are subtle, and the unsuspecting parent is surprised when the teacher talks about the child's poor skills at the first conference. Johnny can't remember the alphabet letters that have been introduced; he may be having trouble with the letters in his name; his fine motor skills are poor; he avoids coloring and cutting; his balance is off; he has trouble remembering where the top of his paper is; and he is easily distracted when doing visual work. Other more obvious signals include turning or tilting the head or paper; closing or covering one eye when working; red, watering, burning, or itchy eyes; crossed or turned eyes; excessive blinking or rubbing of eyes; or headaches.

These problems should be noticed in kindergarten. If they are not, children will become frustrated when they reach 1st grade, where the real demand on their visual systems begins, with long periods of the day devoted to near-point visual activities such as reading and printing. Some children fall behind and feel unsuccessful, frustrated, and highly stressed. When children feel stressed, they may withdraw, avoid difficult activities, or develop behavior problems. The real key to helping these children is early identification and intervention.

Darren is an example of a child with an undetected visual problem. He was referred for evaluation in 1st grade to determine if he was learning disabled in reading. He couldn't remember letters, had trouble writing his name, and avoided fine-motor tasks. His teacher and parents were worried. The evaluation revealed several things. He was having trouble with visual tracking and convergence. His balance was poor. He refused to do any fine-motor tasks except print his name.

When his parents were asked about his developmental history, they reported that Darren avoided outdoor play. He had fallen from a swing at age 3 and broken his arm. Because of the pain and fear, he did not play outdoors for almost a year. He watched too much television, played video games, and was fairly sedentary. A motor activity program to be done at home was suggested. This program included throwing and catching a ball on a balance board, bilateral activities like running and skipping, and lots of fine-motor play including cutting, puzzles, clay, coloring, Legos, and drawing. His video entertainment time was significantly reduced. In three weeks his mother and teacher were thrilled. He no longer avoided hand-eye activities. He knew all his letters! Soon he was learning words, and by the end of 1st grade he was ready for 2nd grade.

What Can Schools Do to Help?

Schools can certainly help children with visual problems. First, teachers must learn to recognize visual problems in their students, especially those who are struggling. Local developmental optometrists or ophthalmologists may be available to train teachers and parents. Training one staff member in a building to screen for visual problems and be available to work with parents is well worth the money. Academic Therapy Publications offers a comprehensive vision test available to schools that does not require a vision professional to administer (See Richards, 1984). Next, good movement programs beginning in kindergarten or preschool need to be developed. A standard physical education program is not enough to help some children.

At Miller Early Childhood Center in Brighton, Michigan, movement and visual development are a priority. A visual motor integration lab helps children with balance and vision problems. Any child with identified visual development or motor delays attends two or three weekly sessions to do specific exercises that enhance tracking, accommodation, convergence, binocular fusion, eye-hand coordination, or balance. Every classroom has trained Motor Moms, volunteer parents who work with all children two or three times a week to improve balance, laterality, coordination, body aware-ness, and depth perception (Sornson, 2000). The entire staff was trained in Project First Step, a program designed to provide teachers daily classroom activities to enhance gross- and fine-motor and oculomotor skills without giving up valuable instructional time (Johnson & Johnson, 1998). Lists of local vision specialists are provided to parents when appropriate. The assis-tance of service organizations such as the Lions Clubs International is so-licited to help fund projects and assist needy families.

For students to be successful in the early years of school, this careful at-tention to developing movement and visual skills must be only one portion of a comprehensive strategy to help every child succeed. The development of phonemic awareness and other language skills, bilateral-motor and other gross-motor skills, hand-eye and other visual thinking skills, along with so-cial and behavioral skills, must be carefully assessed so that each child can experience success. To successfully provide these experiences to children at risk means working closely with their parents.

WHAT CAN PARENTS DO TO HELP?

Parents play the most important role in ensuring that their children have the visual skills necessary for academic success. First, teachers can educate parents about the importance of good visual development. Many good re-sources are listed at the end of this chapter. You may wish to provide par-ents a copy of Figure 8.1.

FIGURE 8.1

HOW PARENTS CAN HELP YOUNG CHILDREN DEVELOP VISUAL SKILLS

- Provide floor time to encourage crawling, reaching for, and playing with colorful and interesting objects. Spend hours playing with your child on the floor, encouraging him to hold and reach for the toys.
- Hang colorful mobiles and pictures by the crib.
- To encourage crawling, which begins the process of establishing bilateral coordination, avoid prolonged use of playpens, car seats, rolling walkers, and jumper swings.
- Look for day-care settings that encourage and understand the importance of movement. Ask about the amount of television and computer time allowed in a child care setting you are evaluating. The American Academy of Pediatrics (2000) recommends no television for the first two years of life! Excessive television viewing limits vision development, language development, social development, and movement. Many experts agree that young children ages 2–10 should be limited to five hours per week or less of viewing.
- Read to your children. Make books, magazines, and newspapers available in your home. Model reading for both information and enjoyment.
- Encourage balance activities, ball games, and outdoor play. Oculomotor (eye muscle) proficiency is developed from years of practice with gross- and fine-motor activity.
- Play games with your children. Sharing activities like hide and seek, tee-ball, hopscotch, card games, coloring, or playing with puzzles, blocks, and Legos will enhance visual development and build loving relationships. Balance and gross-motor skills build the foundation for fine-motor skills, which build the foundation for oculomotor skills.
- Tell stories, such as a bedtime story that continues for several nights, to build visualization and visual memory skills. Encourage your child to see pictures in his mind and to tell you where you were in the story the previous night.
- Play visual memory games, such as concentration or naming objects hidden under a blanket.
- Make treasure maps and ask children to find things around the house and yard.
- Draw, build with blocks, play board games, and work puzzles with your child to strengthen visual memory. Good visual memory skills are the foundation for early reading skill development. Good readers see pictures in their minds as they read. Good spellers notice if the word "looks" wrong.

For children to be successful learners, we must consciously encourage visual skill development early in life. Together, parents and educators can dramatically increase the odds for academic success.

RESOURCES FOR PARENTS

The Children's Vision Committee of the Oregon Optometric Association. (1992). *The effects of vision on learning and school performance.* Milwaukie, OR: Oregon Optometric Association. 800-922-2045.

Dawkins, H., Edelman, E., & Forkiotis, C. (1990). *The suddenly successful student: How behavioral optometry helps.* Santa Barbara, CA: Vision Extension Inc.

Dennison, P. (1994). *Brain gym.* Ventura, CA: The Educational Kinesiology Foundation. 800-356-2109.

Healy, J. (1998). *Failure to connect: How computers affect our children's minds for better or worse.* New York: Simon and Schuster.

Hannaford, C. (1995). *Smart moves: Why learning is not all in your head.* Arlington, VA: Great Ocean Publishers.

Jensen, E. (1998). *Teaching with the brain in mind.* Alexandria, VA: Association for Supervision and Curriculum Development. 800-933-2723.

Landy, J. M., & Burridge, K. R. (1999). *Fundamental motor skills and movement activities for young children.* Center for Applied Research in Education. http://www.phdirect.com.

Sornson, R. (2001). *The 30 minute motor development program.* Brighton, MI: Sparkling Eyes Publishing. 810-229-0148.

Zion, L. C. (1994). *The physical side of learning: Activities kids need to be successful in school.* Byron, CA: Front Row Experience. 800-524-9091.

REFERENCES

American Academy of Pediatrics. (2000). AAP addresses TV programming for children under age two. http://www.aap.org/advocacy/archives/juntele.htm (8 Jan. 2001).

Richards, R. G. (1984). *Visual skills appraisal.* Novato, CA: Academic Therapy Publications.

Sornson, N. (2000). *Motor moms and dads program.* Brighton, MI: Sparkling Eyes Publishing.

Johnson, T., & Johnson, C. (1998). *Project First Step.* Gobles, MI: First Step Inc. of Michigan.

PUTTING THE LEARNING NEEDS OF CHILDREN FIRST

Edward E. Gickling and Verlinda P. Thompson

There was a period in our history when early learning success for every student was not a priority, and many people tacitly supported a system that allowed some students to succeed and others to drift behind and eventually quit. Those who did well could continue on toward more advanced education, while those who faltered could find success in nonacademic pursuits.

Unfortunately, some of the practices inherent to this "sort and select" type of schooling still exist. In our work as consultants over the years, we have seen educational practices that go a long way toward helping every child succeed, but we have also encountered processes that continue to create problems for young learners.

This chapter reflects our thoughts and observations about key practices and processes that promote or hinder early learning success. The first part addresses three important concepts that promote meaningful learning, while the second part addresses three formidable barriers to learning.

CONCEPTS AND PRACTICES
THAT HELP STUDENTS SUCCEED

We know that each student approaches school activity with different levels of knowledge, experience, and skill, all of which affect their thinking and influence the way they construct meaning. These unique differences provide each student with a base from which to learn. An effective teacher begins with this base and builds upon it to achieve favorable results with each and every student.

MAKING CONNECTIONS

Building upon what a student knows is central to all learning. The human mind constantly seeks to make connections between what is new and what it already knows, and never takes in meaningless data (Wolfe & Brandt, 1998). When students cannot connect new information to what they already know, or when they receive information devoid of context, the data quickly disengage and fade away. Under isolated conditions, the brain forgets new information, which then becomes inaccessible to memory (Crowley & Underwood, 1998). Context, in fact, literally means "to be connected and coherent."

Prior knowledge and personal experience are indispensable to learning. The human mind builds relationships by making sense out of new information, which it takes in through the five senses and actively sifts, analyzes, and synthesizes into meaningful categories. For the information to be useful, it must connect with what the student already knows. Unfortunately, teachers frequently violate this basic concept by bombarding less able students with too much unknown information. It is not uncommon for teachers to admit that certain assignments are too hard for some students, yet they assign them anyway. The large number of unknown words appearing in a passage is another example of this type of overload.

Emotion also is significant in making connections, because it heightens awareness: the stronger the emotions connected with an event, the stronger the memory of that event (Wolfe & Brandt, 1998). If emotions connected with an event are positive, they reinforce the memory of the event. If emotions are negative, however, they can have the opposite effect, causing the brain to downshift and our learning to decrease (Wolfe & Brandt, 1998). As Jensen has stated, emotions such as anger, rage, and hate, along with violent and sarcastic attitudes, all need to be eliminated from the classroom and school environment (D'Arcangelo, 1998). We would also add embarrassment and learning failure to this list.

Sylwester notes that "our emotional system drives our attentional system, which drives learning and memory and everything else that we do" (D'Arcangelo, 1998, p. 25). Our emotional system tells us whether or not things are interesting, important, or enjoyable, and can also affect attention. If students aren't interested in a subject, there is no reason for them to pay attention to instruction; if, however, they are turned on to learning, they can become highly motivated to do so (Jensen, 1998b).

MATCHING CURRICULUM AND INSTRUCTION

Matching curriculum and instruction to the needs of each student is the cornerstone of good teaching. The suitability of the match reflects the difficulty of each task and the student's ability to perform it successfully.

Naturally, the best match is student-centered because it builds on what each student knows and is able to do, particularly during new instruction. A successful match confirms to students that they have the knowledge and skills to do well and motivates them to master each new task (Brokowski, 1990; Meichenbaum & Biemiller, 1990). The key ingredient for a successful match is the teacher's ability to diagnose each student's strengths and weaknesses when designing effective instruction.

Learning activities that are too hard or too easy can hinder student productivity. Those that are too hard require an excessive amount of a teacher's time and are negatively correlated with achievement (Beck, 1989; Romberg, 1980), whereas those that are too easy fail to sufficiently challenge students and are often a waste of time. According to Bodrova, Leong, and Paynter (1999),

> Research suggests that children make the most significant gains in learning when they are presented new concepts and skills that are slightly ahead of what they can do independently. In other words, instruction should challenge the child and aim toward the upper levels of what Vygotsky (1978) calls the 'zone of proximal development.' The trick is to find the match between what the child knows and the optimal degree of assistance needed to move the child toward the next developmental step. (p. 45)

The most effective learning tasks are both familiar and challenging. In his classic work *Foundations of Reading Instruction,* Betts (1946) refers to optimal learning conditions as *instructional levels.* Under these conditions, tasks are realistic, appropriately challenging, and continually successful. Experts continue to agree with this fundamental reading premise (Cunningham & Allington, 1998). According to Betts, "maximum development may be expected when the learner is challenged but not frustrated" (p. 449). For practical purposes, the instructional level is where new learning begins, because it represents the point at which students feel confident about mastering new learning tasks.

Educators can use ratios of new/known data to identify student instructional levels. In studying the effects of vocabulary burden on content reading, Betts (1946) notes that when the number of unknown words in a text exceeds 5 percent, comprehension begins to break down. His research, together with a sampling of other research (Gickling & Armstrong, 1978;

Gill, 1992; and Thompson, Gickling, & Havertape, 1983), supports the fact that students need to be able to easily recognize and understand most words in a reading in order to fully comprehend the material.

At the instructional reading level, students must recognize words by sight at least 93 percent of the time. If students need to use decoding skills and context clues to unlock a few unknown words, these high accuracy rates allow them to do so without disrupting comprehension, which should always remain at 80 percent or higher. When comprehension falls below 80 percent, frustration often sets in.

Teachers should also apply the instructional level concept to practice and rehearsal activities. As a general rule, a ratio of 80 percent known data to 20 percent challenging is about right. Teachers who make certain that their students know approximately 80 percent of the material before adding new information have been instrumental in elevating their students' standardized achievement tests scores year after year (Archer et al., 1987). Effective teachers seem to apply these ratios routinely in their teaching, whether consciously or not.

Although children vary a great deal from one another in their learning abilities, they all want to be successful. This statement does not imply that they should all perform at the same level, but simply that they all want to do well and to receive high marks in relation to their own learning levels. The accuracy and comprehension ratios associated with the instructional level are designed to ensure that students perform well and receive high marks relative to their entry skills.

Perhaps an even more accurate gauge of instructional levels than the ratios discussed above is working memory itself. All learning occurs in working memory. "Working memory is what you are paying attention to at any given point. So everything you are mulling over, making a decision about, or are learning, is at first in working memory" (O'Neil, 1996, p. 8). This part of the brain requires a student's undivided attention but has a limited capacity, and clears itself automatically when interfered with. As illustrated in Figure 9.1, a student's working memory capacity develops with age (Juan Pascuel-Leon, 1970). The figure shows that 3-year-olds can generally retain about one new item in working memory at a time—as opposed to approximately seven items for students 15 and older (Miller, 1956).

An instructional level is defined as an appropriate margin of challenge, which is itself decided by the capacity of a student's working memory. For example, 1st graders can retain about three items at a time in working memory, while 4th and 5th graders can retain about five items at a time (Pascuel-Leon, 1970). The size of each learning set is therefore age-related. This does not mean that 1st graders should be restricted to learning only

FIGURE 9.1
INSTRUCTIONAL LEVEL & WORKING MEMORY

Instructional Level

Definition
Optimal learning conditions in which tasks are realistic, appropriately challenging, and continually successful. Represents the point at which students feel confident about mastering new learning tasks.

Criteria
In General	at least 80 percent known data
Drill and Practice	at least 70 to 85 percent known data
Comprehension	at least 93 to 97 percent known data
Reading	at least 93 percent of words recognizable by sight

Working Memory

Definition
Part of the brain through which all information must initially pass before being organized and stored. Requires a student's undivided attention, but has a limited capacity, and clears itself automatically when interfered with.

Capacity

Age	Number of Items
3	1
5	2
7	3
9	4
11	5
13	6
15	7

three items per lesson, but simply that they have a better chance of learning new material when it is presented in sets of three. Decisions about how to organize and divide material into learning sets are merely starting points. The size of each set, as well as the number of sets that can be taught, depends upon how each individual student responds.

Before information can be organized into categories and stored in a student's brain, it must pass through working memory. When a student's capacity for working memory is overloaded, or when a student's concentration wanes, learning simply breaks down.

INSTRUCTIONAL ASSESSMENT

Instructional assessment accurately determines what each student knows and is able to do so that instruction is matched appropriately to the individual learner. As Rosenfield and Gravois (1996) state, "The goal is to work collaboratively to explore the entry level characteristics of the child so that instruction is pegged at the child's instructional level" (p. 16).

Effective instructional assessment measures what children know, what they can do, and how they think in order to determine student needs instead of focusing on their deficiencies. In fact, there is little advantage in identifying what students do not know or what they are unable to do. When students are comfortable with the learning situation, and when they can link new data to known information, they reinforce the connections between learning and memory (Lowery, 1998).

While some children's responses to teacher questions may appear to be void of thought, they are not meaningless. On the surface they may seem random, but in reality the students are trying to bring meaning to the situation. Instead of looking for weaknesses, educators should look for patterns of performance that will help them understand how each student works and thinks. This information can be gleaned by conversing with the child, observing how the child interacts with each task, and continually sampling performance. Taking these steps can help keep a child's success levels high.

Initial assessment helps identify a student's previous experiences in order to begin instruction, while ongoing assessment during classroom problem solving helps identifies the child's continuous learning needs. The role of assessment in adjusting, moderating, and managing instruction is seldom complete.

CONCEPTS AND PRACTICES THAT HINDER LEARNING SUCCESS FOR SOME CHILDREN

It is no longer acceptable to allow young children who are capable of successful learning to drift behind, flounder, and fail. Unfortunately, though, our educational practices have not caught up with this basic fact. Although we know a great deal about how children learn, various legislative policies and administrative practices create barriers to early learning success that are extraordinarily difficult to surmount. The following impediments to the early learning success of children are largely responsible for instruction that is poorly matched to children's needs, and therefore ineffective.

LOCKSTEP INSTRUCTION

Class placements by chronological age are not essentially unsound; children enjoy being with others their own age. What is upsetting about such placements is the lockstep nature of instruction that frequently occurs. There is real pressure on teachers to cover the curriculum assigned to each grade level. As illustrated by Rosenfield (1987), teachers expect students to board the "curriculum express" and to keep up with the routine pace of instruction. Those who are unable to do so become the casualties of a curriculum that moves too quickly and demands too much of students in relation to their entry skills (Gickling & Havertape, 1981; Hargis, 1982). This type of constant pressure hurts good teachers and hinders the learning success of some children.

Grade-level materials dictate classroom content. The scope and sequence of the curriculum determines the topics that are to be covered each year and the amount of time allotted for teaching each topic or lesson. Although students at each grade level may share the same chronological age, "they do not share the same readiness and learning facility to benefit from curricula so rigidly offered" (Hargis, 1997, p. 7). The curriculum is too often based on grade level and calendar year rather than on the needs of individual students. This sort of inflexibility requires all children to conform to a single mode of instruction, and in the process hurts those students who struggle the most with school, because a single level of instruction is imposed on all children (Hargis, 1997).

To acknowledge that children learn differently and that they enter school at different readiness points is one thing; to match curriculum and instruction to the learning needs of particular students is something else entirely. Once a child enters the public school system, the broad acceptance of readiness and emerging concepts of literacy are seemingly lost to curricular initiatives at both state and district levels. One-size-fits-all instruction, as well as politically mandated testing requirements, becomes the general rule. Children are evaluated by adopted criteria, passed or failed by a lockstep grading system, labeled according to deficiencies, and, in some cases, assigned to special programs. Too often this occurs without any real awareness of what individual children actually know, what they are ready for, and what they are capable of doing.

Based on what we know about student diversity, it is hard to understand why public and private education continue to adhere to a rigid practice of grade-level instruction. At every grade level, student performance extends well below and well above grade-level designations. This fact is overshadowed, though, by the pressures placed on teachers to follow the state and school district's mandated curriculum. The constant friction between the learning needs of students and lockstep curriculum practices makes appropriate instruction for the less-able learner a tenuous goal.

LEARNING READINESS

Another barrier to effective learning involves the concept of readiness. Learning readiness is not confined to a single age or grade level, but spans several years in ability for any age level among children. We typically think of learning readiness in reference to early childhood, though, particularly kindergarten and 1st grade. During these fragile early learning years, students are usually screened for sensory, health, and learning impairments. To the credit of most families, most young children are prepared to learn what is expected of them given their early school experiences, and are able to progress without any real difficulties.

Unfortunately, a significant number of children come to school without the early experiences necessary for success, and therefore quickly fall behind (Snow, Burns, & Griffin, 1998). Educators have typically focused on identifying these students' deficiencies and on determining how far behind they are. Such information has not, however, been very helpful in developing meaningful instructional bridges for these children.

We need to emphasize that learning readiness does not take place solely in early childhood; Figure 9.2 provides a glimpse of its real scope. The range of reading scores illustrates the variability of readiness at each grade level, as well as the extent to which variability increases with age. Such data confirm the fact that readiness is an ongoing issue for every subject area at every grade level. We should think seriously about readiness issues at the first signs of a learning difficulty—at every age and stage of development—so that prevention and early intervention can take place. We want to reinforce that all children are ready to learn, only at different levels. Teachers must determine what the students are actually ready for, and to what degree. One of the more difficult tasks for a teacher is to move back instructionally to where students can achieve successfully, rather than forging ahead in the prescribed curriculum.

If you are beginning to think that age is a poor determiner of learning readiness for a large number of students, you are absolutely right. Chronological-age placements may be administratively convenient, but they do not meet the needs of many children; in fact, they often serve more to frustrate and discourage less able students than to help them. These placements can also leave more able students non-productive and bored.

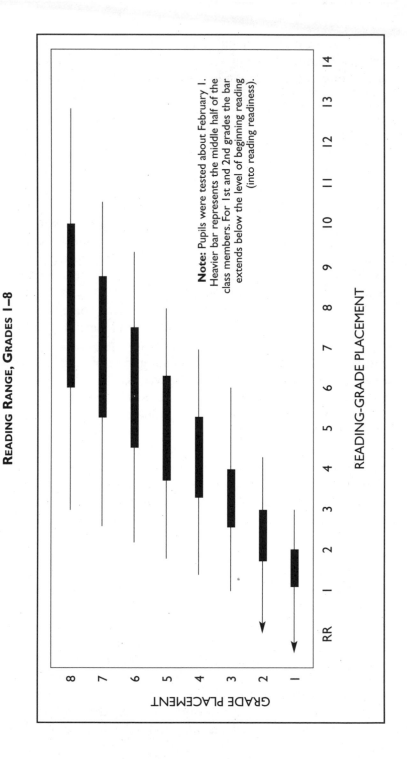

FIGURE 9.2
READING RANGE, GRADES 1–8

Note: Pupils were tested about February 1. Heavier bar represents the middle half of the class members. For 1st and 2nd grades the bar extends below the level of beginning reading (into reading readiness).

READING-GRADE PLACEMENT

GRADE PLACEMENT

AVERAGE OR NORMAL

Those responsible for making educational policies and decisions would seem to prefer that students hail from Garrison Keillor's Lake Wobegon, where "all the children are above average." The performance of children who are below average, no matter the reason, is unacceptable to many. But what does average mean? And more importantly, what does it mean to be normal? The data in Figure 9.2 on page 84 represent but one example of the tremendous variability in the overall reading performance of students.

The series of horizontal lines on the table indicates the reading achievement ranges of students in grades 1–8. A close look at the data shows that the reading achievement scores of these particular students do not conform to a simplistic system of grade-level placement. It is normal for the reading levels of students to span several placement years within each grade, even among the middle 50 percent. For the 1st graders in Figure 9.2, reading achievement ranged from 1st- to 3rd-grade levels. The *median* range actually increased with each succeeding grade, and by the 8th grade spanned as much as ten placement years. Although the data were collected years ago (Carillo, 1964), there is every reason to believe that the performance patterns of today's students are similar. The reading-achievement ranges recorded here are not unusual. They are, in fact, quite normal for schools across the country (Allington & Walmsley, 1995).

The heavier bands of each line in the figure represent the middle 50 percent of each grade level. Except for 1st grade, the ranges represented by these bands span more than a single placement-year achievement level. A comparison of the limited range of the heavier bands with the total span of each line shows that 50 percent of students at each grade level are not "average" learners for their grade. Approximately one-fourth of the students have reading scores that are below average, and another one-fourth have above-average scores.

The figure merely confirms the fact that reading performance varies widely among students at every grade level. There is no reason to expect that these conditions would be much different today, given the increasingly diverse nature of the student population; in fact, an "increasingly diverse" student population might actually produce *greater* variability in performance. Student variability has always been with us. It is normal for students of the same age and grade level to exhibit different abilities and to learn at different rates. The quandary that we now face is that much of society has come to view the performances of those who function below average as abnormal (Hargis, 1990). It is important to note that students whose work is below average also need stimulating instruction, matched to their instructional levels, with extra time given to acquire the basic skills necessary for a lifetime of learning.

STRATEGIES FOR TEACHING AT STUDENTS' INSTRUCTIONAL LEVELS

Students who struggle in school need to be taught at their instructional levels. Working at this level lets the students create bridges between new and known information, and to progress according to their capabilities. The following points can help teachers to keep instructional levels high.

• **Maintain an emotionally positive and safe learning environment.** When students feel intimidated, rejected, threatened, or at risk of failing, their emotional systems can create a downshift in the brain, causing them to focus on self-protection rather than on the lesson at hand. When students feel emotionally supported and successful, however, they are able to remain interested in and excited by learning.

• **Place the needs of students before the needs of content.** If we really believe in child-centered learning, then the learning needs of children must take priority over prescribed state and district curriculum programs. There are far too many student casualties in today's schools, due simply to the inflexible nature of the curriculum. As Hargis (1997) notes, by refusing to address the problems with this type of lockstep orientation, teachers have failed to adequately specify the causes of, or solutions to, instructional problems.

• **Provide appropriate margins of challenge in learning activities.** If the instruction is well beyond the student's level of readiness, stress builds up and learning diminishes. It is worth remembering that if you "want better learning and better learner feelings, then you ought to offer students more learning success and fewer learning errors" (Block, 1980, p. 97). The entry-level values discussed above are designed to ensure high success rates for students relative to what they know and how they perform.

• **Avoid violating the limits of working memory.** Working memory serves to rid the mind of clutter. It has a limited capacity, requires one's undivided attention, and clears itself automatically. Teachers would do well to "chunk" new data into small sets that conform to the limits of working memory. Don't forget: all learning is in working memory, but working memory lasts only seconds unless the new information is repeated continuously.

• **Provide students with time to process new information.** Jensen (1998b) advises teachers to keep their demands for attention to short bursts, no longer than the age of their students in minutes (e.g., seven minutes for 7-year-olds). Teachers should use these bursts to get specific points across, and should intersperse them with time for the students to process the lesson. Jensen recommends that at least half the time allotted for instruction be set aside as processing time. If processing time is not set aside, an awful lot of reteaching—or worse, none at all—may occur.

We know that most children who struggle in school are able to become comfortable and excited about learning when given the chance. All educators are responsible for providing their students with real opportunities for success.

REFERENCES

Allington, R. L., & Walmsley, S. A. (1995). *No quick fix: Rethinking literacy programs in America's elementary schools.* Barksdale, NJ: International Reading Association.

Archer, A. L., Adams, A., Ellis, E. S., Isaacson, S., Morehead, M. K., & Schiller, E. P. (1987). *Working with mildly handicapped students: Design and delivery of academic lessons.* Reston, VA: Council for Exceptional Children.

Beck, I. L. (1989). Improving practices through understanding reading. In L. B. Resnick & L. E. Klopfer (Eds.). *Toward the thinking curriculum: Current cognitive research* (p. 41). Alexandria, VA: Association for Supervision and Curriculum Development.

Betts, E. A. (1946). *Foundations of reading instruction.* New York: American Book.

Block, J. H. (1980). Success rate. In C. Denham & A. Lieberman (Eds.). *Time to learn* (pp. 95–106). Washington, DC: U.S. Department of Education, National Institute of Education.

Bodrova, E., Leong, D. J., & Paynter, D. E. (1999). Literacy standards for preschool learners. *Educational Leadership, 57*(2), 42–46.

Brokowski, J. (1990, May). *Moving metacognition into the classroom.* Paper presented at the Conference on Cognitive Research for Instructional Innovation. College Park, MD: University of Maryland.

Carillo, L. W. (1964). *Informal reading-readiness experiences.* San Francisco: Chandle Publishing Co.

Crowley, G., & Underwood, A. (1998, June 15). Memory. *Newsweek, 131*(24), 48–49, 51–54.

Cunningham, P. M., & Allington, R. L. (1998). *Classrooms that work: They can all read and write.* New York: Addison Wesley Longman, Inc.

D'Arcangelo, M. D. (1998). The brains behind the brain. *Educational Leadership, 56*(3), 20–25.

Gickling, E. E. & Armstrong, D. L. (1978). Levels of instructional difficulty as related to on-task behavior, task completion, and comprehension. *Journal of Learning Disabilities, 11*, 559–566.

Gickling, E. E., & Havertape, J. F. (1981). Curriculum-based assessment. In J. A. Tucker (Ed.). *Non-test based assessment* (CB4/R1–W59). Minneapolis: The National School Psychology Inservice Network, University of Minnesota.

Gill, T. J. (1992). Focus on research: Development of word knowledge as it relates to reading, spelling, and instruction. *Language Arts, 69*, 444–453.

Hargis, C. H. (1982). *Teaching reading to handicapped children.* Denver: Love Publishing.

Hargis, C. H. (1990). *Grades and grading practices: Obstacles to improving education and to helping at-risk students.* Springfield, IL: Charles C. Thomas.

Hargis, C. H. (1997). *Teaching low achieving and disadvantaged students.* Springfield, IL: Charles C. Thomas.

Jensen, E. (1998a). How Julie's brain learns. *Educational Leadership, 56*(3), 41–45.

Jensen, E. (1998b). *Teaching with the brain in mind.* Alexandria, VA: Association for Supervision and Curriculum Development.

Lowery, L. (1998). Curriculum reflects brain research. *Educational Leadership, 56*(3), 27–30.

Meichenbaum, D., & Biemiller, A. (1990, May). *In search of student expertise in the classroom: A metacognitive analysis.* Paper presented at the Conference on Cognitive Research for Instructional Innovation. College Park, MD: University of Maryland.

Miller, C. A. (1956). The magic number seven, plus or minus two: On our capacity for processing information. *The Psychological Review, 63*(2), 81–97.

O'Neil, J. (1996). On emotional intelligence: A conversation with Daniel Goleman. *Educational Leadership, 54*(1), 6–11.

Pascuel-Leon, J. (1970). In P. Wolfe (Ed.). *Mind, memory, and learning: Applying brain research to classroom practice* (p. 12). Allentown, PA: Lehigh Valley Lead Teacher Training Center.

Romberg, T. A. (1980). Salient features of the BTES framework of teacher behavior. In C. Denham & A. Lieberman (Eds.). *Time to learn* (pp. 73–88). Washington, DC: U.S. Department of Education, National Institute of Education.

Rosenfield, S. A. (1987). *Instructional consultation.* Hillsdale, NJ: Lawrence Erlbaum Associates.

Rosenfield, S. A., & Gravois, T. A. (1996). *Instructional consultation teams.* New York: Guilford Press.

Snow, C., Burns, S., & Griffin, P. (Eds.). (1998). *Preventing reading difficulties in young children.* Washington, DC: National Academy Press.

Thompson, V. P., Gickling, E. E., & Havertape, J. F. (1983). The effects of medication and curriculum on task-related behaviors of attention deficit disordered and low achieving peers. *Monograph in behavior disorders: Severe behavior disorders in children and youth.* Tempe, AZ: Council for Children with Behavioral Disorders (CCBD)-Council for Exceptional Children (CEC), Arizona State University.

Wolfe, P., & Brandt, R. (1998). What we do know from brain research. *Educational Leadership, 56*(3), 8–1.

SUCCESS FOR ALL: FAILURE PREVENTION AND EARLY INTERVENTION

Robert E. Slavin

E very September, 3 million children in the United States enter kindergarten. Every one of them is absolutely confident that he or she is going to do well in school. Every one of them is smart and knows it. Every one is highly motivated, eager to learn.

Just two years later, many of these bright, enthusiastic children have learned a hard lesson. Many have failed 1st grade; others barely pass, but are beginning to see that they are not making it. In particular, some students know that they are not reading as well as their classmates. As they proceed through the elementary grades, many students begin to see that they are failing at their full-time jobs. When this happens, things begin to unravel. Failing students begin to have poor motivation and poor self-expectations, which lead to continued poor achievement in a declining spiral that ultimately leads to despair, delinquency, and dropout.

Remediating learning deficits after they are already well established is extremely difficult. Children who have already failed to learn to read, for example, are now anxious about reading, interfering with their ability to focus on it. Their motivation to read may be low. Clearly, the time to provide additional help to children who are at risk is early, when children are still motivated and confident and when any learning deficits are relatively small

Author's note: Portions of this paper were adapted from Slavin, Madden, Dolan, & Wasik, 1996. This paper was written under funding from the Office of Educational Research and Improvement (OERI), U.S. Department of Education (Grant No. OERI-R-117-D40005). However, any opinions expressed are those of the author and do not represent OERI positions or policies.

and remediable. The most important goal in educational programming for students at risk of school failure is to try to make certain that we do not squander the greatest resource we have: the enthusiasm and positive self-expectations of young children themselves.

In practical terms, what this perspective implies is that services for at-risk children must be shifted from an emphasis on remediation to an emphasis on prevention and early intervention. Prevention means providing developmentally appropriate preschool and kindergarten programs so that students will enter 1st grade ready to succeed; and it means providing regular classroom teachers with effective instructional programs, curricula, and staff development to enable them to see that most students are successful the first time they are taught. Early intervention means that these services are provided early in students' schooling and that they are intensive enough to quickly bring at-risk students to a level at which they can profit from good classroom instruction.

This chapter describes the nature and outcomes of a program designed around this vision, a program that emphasizes failure prevention and early, intensive intervention to see that all children in schools serving disadvantaged students are successful in basic skills the first time they are taught, and that they can build on that success throughout the elementary years.

The name of this program is Success for All. The idea behind Success for All is to use everything we know about effective instruction for students at risk to direct all aspects of school and classroom organization toward the goal of preventing academic deficits from appearing in the first place; recognizing and intensively intervening with any deficits that do appear; and providing students with a rich and full curriculum to enable them to build on their firm foundation in basic skills. The commitment of Success for All is to do whatever it takes to see that every child makes it through 3rd grade at or near grade level in reading and other basic skills, and then goes beyond this level in the later grades.

Success for All is currently being implemented in 1,800 schools in 48 states in the United States, reaching about one million students. Almost all these schools are among the most disadvantaged and lowest-achieving schools in their respective districts; most qualify as Title I schoolwide projects, which means that at least 50 percent of the students are in poverty. Many of these schools serve student bodies that are almost 100-percent African American or 100-percent Hispanic, although many are integrated. The schools are located in all parts of the United States, in rural as well as urban settings. Adaptations of the program are also being implemented in Canada, Australia, Israel, and Mexico.

OVERVIEW OF SUCCESS FOR ALL COMPONENTS

Success for All has somewhat different components at different sites, depending on the school's needs and resources available to implement the program. However, there is a common set of elements characteristic of all (adapted from Slavin et al., 1996).

READING PROGRAM

Success for All uses a reading curriculum based on research and effective practices in beginning reading (e.g., Adams, 1990), and on effective use of cooperative learning (Slavin, 1995; Stevens, Madden, Slavin, & Farnish, 1987).

Reading teachers at every grade level begin the reading time by reading children's literature to students and engaging them in a discussion of the story to enhance their understanding of the story, and to build their listening and speaking vocabulary and knowledge of story structure. In kindergarten and 1st grade, the program emphasizes the development of oral language and prereading skills through the use of thematically based units that incorporate areas such as language, art, and writing under a science or social studies topic. A component called Story Telling and Retelling (STaR) involves the students in listening to, retelling, and dramatizing children's literature. Large-print books, as well as oral and written composing activities, allow students to develop concepts of print as they also develop knowledge of story structure. There is also a strong emphasis on phonetic awareness activities, which help develop auditory discrimination and support the development of reading readiness strategies.

Reading Roots is typically introduced in the second semester of kindergarten or in 1st grade. This K–1 beginning reading program uses as its base a series of phonetically regular but meaningful and interesting minibooks and emphasizes repeated oral reading to partners as well as to the teacher. The minibooks begin with a set of "shared stories," in which part of a story is written in small type (read by the teacher) and part is written in large type (read by the students). The student portion uses a phonetically controlled vocabulary. Taken together, the teacher and student portions create interesting, worthwhile stories. Over time, the teacher portion diminishes and the student portion lengthens, until students are reading the entire book. This scaffolding allows students to read interesting literature when they have only a few letter sounds.

Letters and letter sounds are introduced in an active, engaging set of activities that begin with oral language and move into written symbols. Individual sounds are integrated into a context of words, sentences, and stories. Instruction is provided in story structure, specific comprehension skills, metacognitive strategies for self-assessment and self-correction, and integration of reading and writing.

Spanish bilingual programs use an adaptation of Reading Roots called Lee Conmigo ("Read With Me"). Lee Conmigo employs the same instructional strategies as Reading Roots, but uses Spanish reading materials.

When students reach the second reading level, they use a program called Reading Wings, an adaptation of Cooperative Integrated Reading and Composition (CIRC) (Stevens et al., 1987). Reading Wings uses cooperative learning activities built around story structure, prediction, summarization, vocabulary building, decoding practice, and story-related writing. Students engage in partner reading and structured discussion of stories or novels, and work in teams toward mastery of the vocabulary and content of the story. Story-related writing is also shared within teams. Cooperative learning both increases students' motivation and engages students in cognitive activities known to contribute to reading comprehension, such as elaboration, summarization, and rephrasing (see Slavin, 1995). Research on CIRC has found that it significantly increases students' reading comprehension and language skills (Stevens et al., 1987).

In addition to these story-related activities, teachers provide direct instruction in reading comprehension skills, and students practice these skills in their teams. Classroom libraries of trade books at students' reading levels are provided for each teacher, and students read books of their choice for homework for 20 minutes each night. Home readings are shared via presentations, summaries, puppet shows, and other formats twice a week during "book club" sessions.

Materials to support Reading Wings through the 6th grade (or beyond) exist in English and Spanish. The materials are built around children's literature and the most widely used basal series and anthologies. Supportive materials have been developed for more than 100 children's novels and for most current basal series.

Beginning in the second semester of program implementation, Success for All schools usually implement a writing and language arts program based primarily on cooperative learning principles (see Slavin, Madden, & Stevens, 1989/90).

Students in grades 1 to 6 are regrouped for reading. The students are assigned to heterogeneous, age-grouped classes most of the day, but during a regular 90-minute reading period they are regrouped by reading performance levels into reading classes in which all students are at the same level. For example, a 2-1 reading class might contain 1st-, 2nd-, and 3rd-grade students all reading at the same level. The reading classes are smaller than homerooms because tutors and other certified staff (such as librarians or art teachers) teach reading during this common reading period. Re-grouping allows teachers to teach the whole reading class without having to break the class into reading groups. This arrangement greatly reduces the time spent in seatwork and increases direct instruction time, eliminating workbooks, dittos, or other follow-up activities needed in classes that have multiple reading groups.

EIGHT-WEEK READING ASSESSMENTS

At eight-week intervals, reading teachers assess student progress through the reading program. The results of the assessments are used to determine who is to receive tutoring, to change students' reading groups, to suggest other adaptations in students' programs, and to identify students who need other types of assistance, such as family interventions or screening for vision and hearing problems. The assessments are curriculum-based measures that include teacher observations and judgments as well as more formal measures of reading comprehension.

READING TUTORS

One of the most important elements of the Success for All model is the use of tutors to promote students' success in reading. One-to-one tutoring is the most effective form of instruction known (see Wasik & Slavin, 1993). The tutors are certified teachers with experience teaching Title I, special education, and/or primary reading. Often, well-qualified paraprofessionals also tutor children with less severe reading problems. In this case, a certified tutor monitors their work and assists with the diagnostic assessment and intervention strategies. Tutors work one-to-one with students who are having difficulties keeping up with their reading groups. The tutoring occurs in 20-minute sessions during times other than reading or math periods.

In general, tutors support students' success in the regular reading curriculum, rather than teaching different objectives. For example, the tutor will work with a student on the same story and concepts being read and taught in the regular reading class; however, tutors seek to identify learning problems and use different strategies to teach the same skills. They also teach metacognitive skills beyond those taught in the classroom program.

Schools may have as many as six or more teachers serving as tutors, depending on school size, the need for tutoring, and other factors.

During daily 90-minute reading periods, certified tutors serve as additional reading teachers to reduce class size for reading. Reading teachers and tutors use brief forms to communicate about students' specific problems and needs and meet at regular times to coordinate their approaches with individual children.

Initial decisions about reading group placement and the need for tutoring are based on informal reading inventories that the tutors give to each child. Subsequent reading group placements and tutoring assignments are made using the curriculum-based assessments described previously. First-graders receive priority for tutoring, on the assumption that the primary function of the tutors is to help all students be successful in reading the first time, before they fail and become remedial readers.

PRESCHOOL AND KINDERGARTEN

Most Success for All schools provide a half-day preschool and/or a full-day kindergarten for eligible students. The preschool and kindergarten programs focus on providing a balanced and developmentally appropriate learning experience for young children. The curriculum emphasizes the development and use of language. It provides a balance of academic readiness and nonacademic music, art, and movement activities in a series of thematic units. Readiness activities include use of a language development program and Story Telling and Retelling (STaR) in which students retell stories read by the teachers. Prereading activities begin during the second semester of kindergarten.

FAMILY SUPPORT TEAM

Parents are an essential part of the formula for success in Success for All. A family support team works in each school, serving to make families feel comfortable in the school and become active supporters of their children's education as well as providing specific services. The family support team consists of the school's parent liaison, vice principal (if any), counselor (if any), facilitator, and any other appropriate staff already present in the school or added to the school staff.

The Family support team first works to establish good relations with parents and to increase involvement in the schools. Family support team members may complete "welcome" visits for new families. They organize many attractive programs in the school, such as parenting skills workshops.

Many schools use a program called Raising Readers, in which parents are given strategies to use in reading with their own children.

The family support team also intervenes to solve problems. For example, they may contact parents whose children are frequently absent to see what resources can be provided to assist the family in getting their child to school. Family support staff, teachers, and parents work together to solve school behavior problems. Also, family support staff are called on to provide assistance when students seem to be working at less than their full potential because of problems at home. Families of students who are not receiving adequate sleep or nutrition, need glasses, are not attending school regularly, or are exhibiting serious behavior problems may receive family support assistance.

The family support team is strongly integrated into the academic program of the school. It receives referrals from teachers and tutors regarding children who are not making adequate academic progress, and thereby constitutes an additional stage of intervention for students in need above and beyond that provided by the classroom teacher or tutor. The family support team also encourages and trains the parents to fulfill numerous volunteer roles within the school, from providing a listening ear for emerging readers to helping in the school cafeteria.

Program Facilitator

A program facilitator works at each school to oversee (with the principal) the operation of the Success for All model. The facilitator helps plan the Success for All program, helps the principal with scheduling, and visits classes and tutoring sessions frequently to help teachers and tutors with individual problems. She works directly with the teachers on implementation of the curriculum, classroom management, and other issues; helps teachers and tutors deal with any behavior problems or other special problems; and coordinates the activities of the family support team with those of the instructional staff.

Teachers and Teacher Training

The teachers and tutors are regular certified teachers. They receive detailed teacher's manuals supplemented by three days of inservice training at the beginning of the school year. For classroom teachers of grades 1–5 and for reading tutors, these training sessions focus on implementation of the reading program, and their detailed teachers' manuals cover general teaching strategies as well as specific lessons. Preschool and kindergarten teachers and aides are trained in use of the STaR and Peabody programs, thematic units, and other aspects of the preschool and kindergarten models. Tutors later receive two additional days of training on tutoring strategies and reading assessment.

Throughout the year, additional inservice presentations are made by the facilitators and other project staff on such topics as classroom management, instructional pace, and cooperative learning. Facilitators also organize many informal sessions to allow teachers to share problems and solutions, suggest changes, and discuss individual children. The staff development model used in Success for All emphasizes relatively brief initial training with extensive classroom follow-up, coaching, and group discussion.

FUNDING

Most funds to support implementation of Success for All are reallocations of Title I funds that high-poverty schools would typically receive whether or not they are implementing the program. Traditionally, Title I money has overwhelmingly supported remedial teachers and classroom aides. Success for All typically uses these positions in different ways (as teachers and facilitators), rather than adding resources to the school. In addition to Title I, many schools incorporate funding from sources such as special education, bilingual education, and state funds for high-poverty schools.

RELENTLESSNESS

While the particular elements of Success for All may vary from school to school, there is one feature we try to make consistent: a relentless focus on the success of every child. It would be entirely possible to have tutoring, curriculum change, family support, and other services, yet still not ensure the success of at-risk children. Success does not come from piling on additional services but from coordinating human resources around a well-defined goal, constantly assessing progress toward that goal, and never giving up until success is achieved.

None of the elements of Success for All is completely new or unique to this program. What is most distinctive about the program is its schoolwide, coordinated, and proactive plan for translating positive expectations into concrete success for all children. All children can complete elementary school reading confidently, strategically, and joyfully and can maintain the enthusiasm and positive self-expectations with which they entered kindergarten. The purpose of Success for All is to see that this vision can become a practical reality in every school.

RESEARCH ON SUCCESS FOR ALL •

From the beginning, there has been a strong focus in Success for All on research and evaluation. Evaluations have compared Success for All schools to matched comparison schools on measures of reading performance, starting with cohorts in kindergarten or in 1st grade and continuing to follow these students as long as possible. Vagaries of funding and other local problems have ended some evaluations prematurely, but most have been able to follow Success for All schools for many years. As of this writing, there are seven years of continuous data from the six original schools in Baltimore and Philadelphia, and varying numbers of years of data from nine other districts, a total of 29 schools (and their matched control schools).

In all cases, reading tests were administered by testers who were unaffiliated with the project. Every attempt was made to keep testers unaware of whether a school was a Success for All school or a control school. Testers were trained to a high degree of reliability and then observed on a sampling basis to be sure they were administering the tests properly.

Each of the evaluations follows children who began in Success for All in 1st grade or earlier, in comparison to children who had attended the control school over the same period. For more details on methods and findings, see Slavin and Madden (2001).

READING OUTCOMES

The results of the multi-site replicated experiment evaluating Success for All are summarized in Figure 10.1, which incorporates data from about 3,000 students. Statistically significant ($p = .05$ or better) positive effects of Success for All (compared to controls) were found on every measure at every grade level, 1–5. In addition, positive effects were maintained into grades 6 and 7, when children had gone on to middle school. Effects sizes for students in the lowest 25 percent of their grades were particularly positive, as were effects for limited-English-proficient students (see Slavin & Madden, 1999b).

Several studies have found substantial reductions in special education placements in Success for All schools, as well as improvements in the achievement of children categorized as learning disabled (Slavin, 1996; Smith, Ross, & Casey, 1994).

Two studies found a strong relationship between the degree of program implementation and student outcomes (Nunnery et al., in press; Ross et al., 1997).

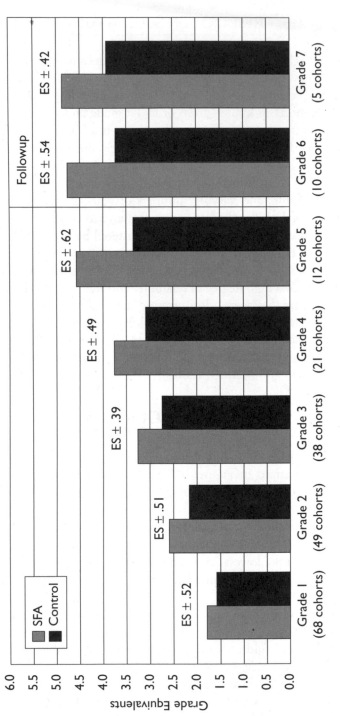

FIGURE 10.1

**COMPARISON OF SUCCESS FOR ALL AND CONTROL SCHOOLS IN MEAN READING GRADE EQUIVALENTS AND EFFECT SIZES
1988–1999**

Note: Effect size (ES) is the proportion of a standard deviation by which Success for All students exceeded controls. Includes approximately 6000 children in Success for All or control schools since first grade.

In recent years, programs in mathematics, science, and social studies have been added to the Success for All reading program to create a comprehensive design called Roots & Wings. Evaluations of the full Roots & Wings model are showing positive effects on measures of achievement in all academic areas, including mathematics, science, and social studies (Slavin & Madden, 1999c).

CONCLUSION

The results of evaluations of 23 Success for All schools in nine districts in eight U.S. states clearly show that the program increases student reading performance. In every district, Success for All students learned significantly more than matched control students. Significant effects were not seen on every measure at every grade level, but the consistent direction and magnitude of the effects show unequivocal benefits for Success for All students. Evidence showed particularly large effects on the achievement of limited-English-proficient students in both bilingual and ESL programs, and on both reducing special education referrals and improving the achievement of students who have been assigned to special education.

An important indicator of the robustness of Success for All is the fact that of the more than 1,100 schools that have used the program for periods of 1–8 years, only about 30 have dropped out (usually because of changes of principals). Many other Success for All schools have survived changes of superintendents, principals, facilitators, and other key staff; major cuts in funding; and other serious threats to program maintenance.

The demonstration that an effective program can be replicated and can be effective in its replication sites removes one more excuse for the continuing low achievement of disadvantaged children. To ensure the success of disadvantaged students, we must have the political commitment to do so, with the funds and policies to back up this commitment. Success for All does require a serious commitment to restructure elementary schools and to reconfigure uses of funds to emphasize failure prevention and early intervention rather than remediation. These and other systemic changes in assessments, accountability, standards, and legislation can facilitate the implementation of Success for All and other school reform programs. However, we must also have methods known not only to be effective in their original sites, but also to be replicable and effective in other sites.

Clearly, preventing children from experiencing academic problems makes far more sense than allowing them to fall behind and only then providing remedial or special education services. Success for All provides one demonstration that failure prevention and early intervention can make a substantial difference in the school success of at-risk children.

REFERENCES

Adams, M. J. (1990). *Beginning to read: Thinking and learning about print.* Cambridge, MA: MIT Press.

Nunnery, J., Slavin, R. E., Ross, S. M., Smith, L. J., Hunter, P., & Stubbs, J. (1996, April). *An assessment of Success for All program component configuration effects on the reading achievement of at-risk first grade students.* Paper presented at the annual meeting of the American Educational Research Association, New York.

Ross, S. M., Smith, L. J., & Casey, J. P. (1997). Preventing early school failure: Impacts of Success for All on standardized test outcomes, minority group performance, and school effectiveness. *Journal of Education for Students Placed at Risk, 2*(1), 29–53.

Slavin, R. E. (1995). *Cooperative learning: Theory, research, and practice* (2nd ed.). Boston: Allyn and Bacon.

Slavin, R. E. (1996). Neverstreaming: Preventing learning disabilities. *Educational Leadership, 53*(5), 4–7.

Slavin, R. E., & Madden, N. A. (1999a). *Success for All/Roots & Wings: 1999 summary of research on achievement outcomes.* Baltimore: Johns Hopkins University, Center for Research on the Education of Students Placed at Risk.

Slavin, R. E., & Madden, N. A. (1999b). Effects of bilingual and English as a second language adaptations of Success for All on the reading achievement of students acquiring English. *Journal of Education for Students Placed at Risk, 4*(4).

Slavin, R. E., & Madden, N. A. (1999c). *Roots and wings: Effects of whole-school reform on student achievement.* Baltimore: Johns Hopkins University, Center for Research on the Education of Students Placed at Risk.

Slavin, R. E., & Madden, N. A. (Eds.). (2001). *One million children: Success for All.* Thousand Oaks, CA: Corwin Press.

Slavin, R. E., Madden, N. A., Dolan, L. J., & Wasik, B. A. (1996). *Every child, every school: Success for All.* Newbury Park, CA: Corwin.

Slavin, R. E., Madden, N. A., & Stevens, R. J. (1989/90). Cooperative learning models for the 3 R's. *Educational Leadership, 47*(4), 22–28.

Smith, L. J., Ross, S. M., & Casey, J. P. (1994). *Special education analyses for Success for All in four cities.* Memphis, TN: University of Memphis, Center for Research in Educational Policy.

Stevens, R. J., Madden, N. A., Slavin, R. E., & Farnish, A. M. (1987). Cooperative integrated reading and composition: Two field experiments. *Reading Research Quarterly, 22,* 433–454.

Wasik, B. A., & Slavin, R. E. (1993). Preventing early reading failure with one-to-one tutoring: A review of five programs. *Reading Research Quarterly, 28,* 178–200.

PARENTS AS TEACHERS: IMPROVING THE ODDS WITH EARLY INTERVENTION

Mildred M. Winter

> What we see in the crib is the greatest mind that has ever existed, the most powerful learning machine in the universe.
>
> —*The Scientist in the Crib*

Each week in the United States alone some 77,000 newborns enter the world "born to learn." It's safe to assume that a common hope shared by the parents of these newborns is that their babies will ultimately do well in school and in life.

Early intervention programs launched in the 1960s were designed to respond to that hope. In the late 1960s and early 1970s, some school systems began to use federal Title I funds to help prepare disadvantaged 3- and 4-year-olds for school success. But in Missouri we found that intervention at that age was already late for many children. So in 1981, the Missouri Department of Elementary and Secondary Education decided that to reduce the number of children who enter kindergarten needing special help, educators should support and assist parents in their teaching role from the onset of learning. And thus, the Parents as Teachers (PAT) program was born. Research told us that early human development is a time of both great opportunity and great vulnerability. Investing in good beginnings for children diminishes the probability of having to invest later in social costs such as remedial education, juvenile detainment, welfare dependency, and child abuse and neglect.

CONCEPTUAL FRAMEWORK

Families, schools, and communities share a common goal—to have children become all that they can be. With "beginning at the beginning" as its hallmark, Parents as Teachers was intended as a first step toward that end. The program was designed as a partnership with families, beginning prenatally and extending to age 5. It was based on these two simple truths:

- Babies are born learners.
- Parents play a critical role from the outset in determining what their child will become.

The program was designed for the voluntary participation of families of all configurations, cultural backgrounds, and life circumstances. Now, as then, the major goals are to

- Empower parents to give their children the best possible start in life.
- Provide for early detection of developmental problems.
- Help prepare children for school success.
- Increase parents' feelings of competence and confidence.
- Increase parents' knowledge of child development and appropriate ways to stimulate their child's language, intellectual, social, and motor development.
- Improve parent-child interactions and strengthen family relationships.
- Prevent child abuse and neglect.
- Develop strong home-school-community partnerships for children and families.

Parents as Teachers is based on the following assumptions:

- Parents are the experts on their own children by virtue of their special insight that comes from everyday living with them. They need to be respected as such.
- Whether by accident or design, parents are continually teaching their children through their actions and words.
- Parent educators can work effectively in partnership with parents, offering research-based information on child development and ways to enhance learning.
- Parents do not seek to be "fixed," but rather to learn how to build on their strengths and draw on outside help to benefit their children.

PROGRAM DESCRIPTION

The Parents as Teachers pilot project was launched in 1981 as a cooperative effort of the Missouri Department of Elementary and Secondary Education, four diverse school districts selected on the basis of competitive proposals, and the Danforth Foundation of St. Louis. A total of 380 families who were expecting their first child between December 1981 and September 1982 were enrolled. The families, who were representative of each school district's population, were provided services from the third trimester of pregnancy until the child reached her 3rd birthday. The results of the 1985 independent evaluation of the project's benefits to participating children and parents, as assessed at the children's 3rd birthdays (Pfannenstiel & Seltzer, 1985), led to state funding for implementation of the program in every Missouri school district in 1985–86. A write-up on the program's evaluation results in *The New York Times* in October 1985 led to widespread interest and inquiries from around the world.

Now, as in the pilot project phase, Parents as Teachers offers all families the following services:

• **Personal Visits.** PAT-certified educators, trained in child development and home visiting, help parents understand and develop appropriate expectations for each stage of their child's development. They involve parents in parent-child activities that foster all areas of development and build a strong parent-child relationship. Response to parents' questions and concerns is always a priority during the visits of approximately one hour. Needs of the family and the age of the child determine whether visits are weekly, biweekly, or monthly. Parent materials, written at two reading levels, reinforce and expand upon the information discussed during the visit. Visits are arranged at times convenient to both fathers and mothers so as to accommodate schedules of parents who work outside the home.

• **Group Meetings.** Parents meet to gain new insights and to share their experiences, common concerns, and successes. Group meetings also provide families the opportunity to participate in parent-child activities in a group setting and to build support networks with other families. Many programs also offer families informal drop-in and play times.

• **Developmental Screenings.** Parents as Teachers offers periodic screenings in the areas of development, health, hearing, and vision. The intent is to provide early detection of potential and emerging problems to prevent more serious difficulties later, as well as to reassure parents whose children's development is age-appropriate.

• **Resource Network.** Families are helped to access other needed community services that the program cannot provide. Parents as Teachers has never claimed to be all things to all families.

Adaptability is key to the success of Parents as Teachers. While it is an international model with a comprehensive curriculum and professional training program, it is truly a local program. It can be offered as a stand-alone program or as part of a comprehensive early education and family support system of services. It works well in Even Start and other Title I programs, Early Head Start, Head Start, and programs for teen parents. Although the majority of Parents as Teachers programs are sponsored by school districts, the program has been adapted successfully for child care centers, Bureau of Indian Affairs schools, military bases, and the workplace.

BORN TO LEARN CURRICULUM

The wealth of information the scientific community is producing about the development of the brain and its link to behavior underscores the undeniable importance of children's earliest experiences for brain development. The human brain has a remarkable capacity to learn and change throughout the life span, but there are critical periods that represent unique opportunities to physically affect the brain. A number of these sensitive periods occur during the first three years of life. This knowledge prompted us at the Parents as Teachers National Center (PATNC), with a grant from the Charles A. Dana Foundation, to undertake the task of demystifying brain research findings for parents and other early educators. In 1996, PATNC initiated a collaboration with a team of neuroscientists from the Washington University School of Medicine in St. Louis, Missouri, to bridge the gap between neuroscience and education. Our neuroscience-infused Born to Learn Curriculum resulted, taking this frontier of science from the laboratory to the living room.

The Born to Learn Curriculum consists of written and audiovisual materials for parents and parent educators that translate brain research information into concrete "when," "what," "how," and "why" advice for parents. The neuroscience information gives added credibility to child development and parenting information—it gives the "why" behind the suggestions provided by parent educators. The written materials, which were critiqued by the medical team, include detailed home visit plans, child development and neuroscience information for parents, suggested parent-child activities, and resource materials for parent educators. Personal visit plans are designed for weekly, biweekly, or monthly visits, depending on the needs of individuals and programs.

An international-award-winning video series, funded by the McCormick Tribune Foundation, is an integral part of the curriculum. The videos present neuroscience information keyed to topics parent educators will discuss with parents during personal visits. They feature short presentations by neuroscientists, physicians, and child development professionals using easy-to-understand language. All scripts were reviewed by the neuroscientists for scientific accuracy.

The Born to Learn Curriculum has been field tested with families for whom parenting is a special challenge in St. Louis and Chicago and on five Native American reservation sites. The response from parents and parent educators has been overwhelmingly positive. As of 1999, this curriculum became the standard prenatal-to-age-3 curriculum for PAT programs everywhere. The parent materials and the video series are available in English and Spanish, and translation of the entire curriculum into Spanish is in progress. In response to requests both from parents and parent educators, the addition of neuroscience information to the curriculum for Parents as Teachers for Ages Three to Five is underway.

Proven Effectiveness

True success is measured in terms of changed lives; hence, the challenge to continually evaluate the effectiveness of the Parents as Teachers program. Independent evaluation studies vary extensively in their sample sizes, types of outcome indicators, and use of comparison groups. Some have investigated Parents as Teachers as a stand-alone program, while others have looked at it as part of a more comprehensive initiative. Some of these investigations are described below.

An independent evaluation of the PAT pilot project showed that by age 3, participating children were significantly advanced over their peers in language, social development, problem solving, and other intellectual abilities. PAT parents were more knowledgeable about child rearing practices and child development (Pfannenstiel & Seltzer, 1985).

A follow-up study of the pilot project showed that PAT children scored significantly higher than comparison group children on standardized measures of reading and math achievement in 1st grade. A significantly higher proportion of PAT parents initiated contacts with teachers and took an active role in their child's schooling (Pfannenstiel, 1989).

In 1991, a "Second Wave" study was conducted to determine how well the model program would transfer statewide. Results of the Second Wave evaluation of the PAT program's effect on 400 randomly selected families in 37 diverse school districts across Missouri indicated that both children and parents benefitted. At age 3, PAT children performed significantly above the national norms on measures of intellectual and language abilities, despite the Second Wave sample being overrepresented on all traditional characteristics of risk. More than half the children with observed developmental delays overcame them by age 3. Parent knowledge of child development and appropriate parenting practices increased for all types of families. There were only two documented cases of child abuse in the 400 families during the three-year study period (Pfannenstiel, Lambson, and Yarnell (1991).

A 1993 study of 516 students entering kindergarten in 22 rural school districts in southwest Missouri showed that children who had participated in PAT scored significantly higher on the Kindergarten Inventory of Developmental Skills (KIDS) than those who did not participate. Of the sample, 224 came from economically disadvantaged families (Wheeler, 1994).

A series of studies in Binghamton, New York, beginning in 1992, showed that PAT graduates tested in prekindergarten and again in kindergarten had significantly higher cognitive, language, motor, and social skills than nonparticipants. These advanced skills led to higher grades in kindergarten and lower remedial and special education costs in 1st grade. PAT families also had substantially reduced welfare dependence and half the number of suspected child abuse and neglect cases compared with comparison group families. When assessed again in 2nd grade, PAT children continued to perform better on standardized tests and to require fewer remedial and special education placements (Drazen & Haust, 1995, 1996).

Results of a study in North Carolina of sustained educational effects of the Rutherford County Schools PAT program were reported in 1996. Twenty-one families participated fully in the program for three years; 22 received only a quarterly newsletter during the child's first three years; a third group of 22 families received no services from the school district. At kindergarten entry, the PAT children scored significantly higher than the comparison groups on measures of language and self-help/social skills (Coleman, Rowland, & Hutchins, 1997).

A longitudinal study by the Parkway School District, a large suburban district in St. Louis County, Missouri, reported that 3rd-graders who had been in the program with screening services from birth to age 3 scored significantly higher on the Stanford Achievement Test than nonparticipating counterparts. PAT graduates were less likely to receive remedial reading assistance or be retained in grade. The sample was followed-up in 4th grade, and the PAT graduates continued to significantly outperform non-PAT children on the Stanford Achievement Test (Coates, 1996). The district concluded the study at that point, feeling that the program had proven its worth.

Findings from a state school readiness assessment project conducted in Missouri in 1998 show that Parents as Teachers achieves its goal of preparing children for success in school. The study involved 3,500 kindergarteners from a stratified random sample of school districts and schools across Missouri. Kindergarten teachers in the more than 80 sample schools were trained to rate children's preparation for kindergarten using a 65-item School Entry Profile. Children were rated based on teacher observations after six weeks of school. Parents completed a survey on their child, on which they reported on health issues, the child's participation in child care or preschool, and the frequency and kinds of home literacy activities.

Among children whose care and education were solely home-based, those whose families participated in PAT scored significantly higher on the School Entry Profile. Among children who participated in PAT and attended preschool, both minority and nonminority children, as well as children who attended high-poverty and low-poverty schools, scored above average. Children in all categories who rated above average lived in homes where parents reported above-average frequency of home literacy activities, such as those emphasized in all PAT programs (Missouri Department of Elementary and Secondary Education, 1999).

A multisite study being conducted by SRI International with high-needs families in three metropolitan areas is an evaluation in progress. Families were randomly assigned to either a treatment group receiving PAT services or a no-treatment control group. The study is assessing children's development and parents' knowledge of child development, attitudes toward parenting, and use of appropriate support. Results will be available in the fall of 2001.

COST-EFFECTIVENESS

The positive outcomes of numerous evaluations of Parents as Teachers underscore another important aspect of the program—its cost-effectiveness. A major source of savings to school districts is the elimination of special education services for many children who might otherwise have needed them were it not for their family's participation in PAT. The Parkway School District in St. Louis County, referenced earlier, reports a cost difference of

$6,912 per child per year between regular and special education, or a cumulative savings per child for the K–12 years of $89,856. Studies also indicate that PAT children are less likely to be retained in grade.

Parents as Teachers is also effective in serving teen parents, helping them understand their child's development and the importance of their role—both prenatally and after the baby is born—and supporting them in their effort to continue their education and graduate from high school. These education efforts produce considerable savings to communities at large; teens' increased access to prenatal care leads to a reduction in the number of low-birth-weight babies, who are typically at risk for health problems and developmental delays. By staying in school, teenage mothers not only increase their own ability to stay off welfare and be gainfully employed, but they also increase their child's likelihood of success in school.

Part of the program's appeal is its low cost, the major expense being the salary and travel of parent educators, many of whom work on a part-time basis. This schedule provides added flexibility for personal visits on Saturdays, evenings, early mornings, and lunch times. At most sites, the program does not require extensive facilities or a large investment in materials. Parents are encouraged to take advantage of learning opportunities that occur in everyday living, using materials that are ordinarily found in the home. School districts and other sponsoring agencies commonly make in-kind contributions, such as office and group meeting space, clerical assistance, and program supervision. Annual reports submitted by PAT programs nationally indicate an average expenditure of $1,000–$1,500 per family per year. The frequency of personal visits provided obviously affects cost. One PAT benefit to schools, which has been widely documented but is difficult to translate into dollars, is the marked increase in parent support involvement in education.

CONCLUSION

Evidence of the effectiveness of Parents as Teachers and its affordability have been integral to the expansion of the program. As of the end of 2000, there were 2,655 PAT sites across the United States and in Australia, Canada, Great Britain, Japan, Malaysia, the Northern Mariana Islands, New Zealand, Puerto Rico, the South Pacific Islands, the Virgin Islands, and the West Indies.

It has been said that the first years last forever. Through the Parents as Teachers program, we are working to make them the best years for our children, particularly those who are most vulnerable to failure.

Further information on the Parents as Teachers program is available from:

Parents as Teachers National Center, Inc.
10176 Corporate Square Drive
St. Louis, Missouri, 63132
Telephone 314-432-4330; fax 314-432-8963; e-mail mwint@patnc.org;
   web http://www.patnc.org

REFERENCES

Coates, D. (1996). *Early childhood evaluation*. A report to the Parkway School District Board of Education, Chesterfield, MO.

Coleman, M., Rowland, B., & Hutchins, B. (1997, November). *Parents as teachers: Policy implications for early school intervention*. Paper presented at the annual meeting of the National Council on Family Relations, Crystal City, VA.

Drazen, S., & Haust, M. (1995). *The effects of the Parents and Children Together (PACT) program on school achievement*. Binghamton, NY: Community Resource Center.

Drazen, S., & Haust, M. (1996). *Lasting academic gains from an early home visitation program*. Binghamton, NY: Community Resource Center.

Gopnik, A., Meltzoff, A., & Kuhl, P. (1999). *The scientist in the crib*. NY: William Morrow.

Missouri Department of Elementary and Secondary Education. (1999). *School entry assessment project: Report of findings*. Jefferson City, MO: Author.

Pfannenstiel, J. (1989). *New Parents as Teachers project: A follow-up investigation*. Overland Park, KS: Research & Training Associates.

Pfannenstiel, J., Lambson, T., & Yarnell, V. (1991). *Second wave study of the Parents as Teachers program*. Overland Park, KS: Research & Training Associates.

Pfannenstiel, J., & Seltzer, D. (1985). *Evaluation report: New Parents as Teachers project*. Overland Park, KS: Research & Training Associates.

Pfannenstiel, J., & Seltzer, D. (1989). New parents as teachers: Evaluation of an early parent education program. *Early Childhood Research Quarterly, 4*, 1–18.

Shore, R. (1997). *Rethinking the brain: New insights into early development*. New York: Families and Work Institute.

Wheeler, W. (1994). *A study of the Missouri Parents as Teachers program and its effects on the readiness skills of children entering kindergarten in southwest Missouri public schools*. Blue Eye, MO: Blue Eye School District.

Winter, M. (1995). *Home visiting: Forging the home-school connection*. Washington, DC: U.S. Department of Education.

GETTING READY FOR SCHOOL IN PRESCHOOL

Lawrence J. Schweinhart

The circumstances and events of early childhood stand at the beginning of life, affecting all that follows. This fact is so obvious that even partial denials of it ought to require explanation. Instead, early childhood advocates have assumed the burden of proof, celebrating the findings of program effects and brain research. Perhaps the simple fact of early childhood primacy has become disputed because the confidence it inspires can easily become overconfidence. Life is complex. All human behavior, including the complex sets of behavior involved in school and life success, has a thousand causes, and the ones closest to the act itself are easiest to relate to it. Seeing the roots of adult behavior in early childhood requires a perceptive vision that easily expands into exuberant speculation, a sort of reverse fortune-telling. Careful research on the long-term effects of early childhood programs accurately calibrates our expectations and shows us where to strike the best balance between optimism and pessimism.

Then there is the fact that school begins at age 5 or 6 just about everywhere in the world. Societies equate school with reading, writing, and arithmetic, and these written-symbol processing abilities arise at that age. But to engage in early childhood education, one needs a broader definition of what learning is all about—a definition that encompasses sensory experience as well as reading, writing, and arithmetic. Some people readily embrace this new definition, while others insist on the old, narrow one.

EFFECTS OF GOOD PRESCHOOL PROGRAMS

Hunt (1961) and Piaget (1960) supplied such a new definition in the 1960s by focusing on the emergence of children's logical thinking. Bloom (1964) underscored the importance of early childhood as a time of variability in young children's performance on intelligence tests. Such thinking led Susan Gray and her colleagues to initiate the Early Training Project in Tennessee and David Weikart and his colleagues to initiate the High/Scope Perry Preschool Program in Michigan in 1962, programs which were the subjects of experimentally designed evaluations of their effects on young children born in poverty; these programs initially targeted improvement in intellectual performance as the measure of their success.

Both studies found that their programs improved young children's intellectual performance (IQ) by about 10 points at school entry (Klaus & Gray, 1968; Weikart, Deloria, Lawser, & Wiegerink, 1970). But then, both studies found that this IQ advantage lasted only a couple of years. Many other studies that followed came to the same conclusions (McKey et al., 1985), including the infamous Westinghouse evaluation of Head Start (Westinghouse Learning Corporation, 1969). Permanent improvement in intellectual performance proved to be an unsatisfactory rationale for preschool programs for young children living in poverty. In retrospect, it should not have been surprising that intelligence tests did not assess program effects very well: They were not designed to do so, but rather to be resistant to environmental variation.

Even as this fadeout of intellectual effects was taking place, a new outcome variable was being used to accumulate data—years spent in special education classes or retained in grade. Ironically, it was just such placements that intelligence tests were originally designed to inform. The High/Scope Perry Preschool Study first found such an effect (Weikart, Bond, & McNeil, 1978), and was later corroborated by other studies, including several in the Consortium for Longitudinal Studies (1983), a group formed specifically to look for long-term effects of exemplary preschool programs.

The High/Scope Perry Preschool Study has led the quest for ever longer-term program effects, identifying many long-term effects of preschool programs for young children living in poverty when they reached age 15 (Schweinhart & Weikart, 1980), age 19 (Berrueta-Clement, Schweinhart, Barnett, Epstein, & Weikart, 1984), and age 27 (Schweinhart, Barnes, & Weikart, 1993). The study continues, with data currently being collected at ages 39 to 41.

Despite the fadeout of the program effect on intellectual performance, evidence of the program group's greater school success was abundant. The program group had much higher reading, language, arithmetic, and overall achievement test scores at age 14, as well as higher high school grade-point averages (2.1 versus 1.7 on a four-point scale). The program group did better in reading and general literacy at age 19 and in problem solving at age 27. Program-group parents had higher educational aspirations for their children at age 15 and found them more willing to talk about school. Fewer program-group parents were called in to talk to the teachers about their children's school work. As teens, the program group had a better attitude toward school and reported doing more homework than the no-program group.

Program group members spent an average 1.1 years in treatment for educable mental impairment, as compared to 2.8 years for the no-program group. In contrast, the program group spent an average 1.0 year in compensatory education as compared to 0.4 year for the no-program group. This was probably a less extreme treatment for some of the program-group children, who might otherwise have received treatment for mental impairment. On the average, the program group completed nearly one more year of schooling than the no-program group (11.9 versus 11.0). Two out of three program group members (67 percent) graduated from high school on time, as compared to only 45 percent of the no-program group.

The program group achieved greater economic productivity in adulthood than did the no-program group. At age 27, their monthly earnings averaged $1,219 as compared to the no-program group's $766. The employment rate of program females was 80 percent as compared to only 55 percent for no-program females. Only 59 percent of the program group had received social services as adults, while 80 percent of the no-program group had received such services. Almost three times as many program-group members owned their own homes (36 percent versus 13 percent), and more than twice as many owned a second car (30 percent versus 13 percent).

The program group assumed greater social responsibility in adulthood than did the no-program group: half as many criminal arrests by age 27 (averages of 2.3 versus 4.6 arrests); one-fifth as many habitual criminals (7 percent versus 35 percent with 5 or more arrests); and fewer than one-third as many arrested for drug-related offenses (7 percent versus 25 percent). These arrest differences reflected similar, nearly significant, patterns in teacher-rated misconduct in the early elementary years. In addition, five times as many program group females were married at age 27 (40 percent versus 8 percent) and, as a consequence, had fewer out-of-wedlock births (averages of 1.0 versus 1.7 such births per female).

A regularly updated cost-benefit analysis of the program and its findings has most recently indicated a return on investment to taxpayers of $7.16 per dollar invested—public *benefits* of $88,433 per participant as compared to a program *cost* of $12,356 per participant, in 1992 dollars discounted at 3 percent (Barnett, 1996). The benefits come from reduced costs of schooling, welfare, and the justice system; greater tax revenues from participants' earnings; and, most importantly, reduced costs to potential crime victims of $57,585 per preschool program participant.

Results of other studies have also found long-term effects of high-quality preschool programs for young children living in poverty. The Carolina Abecedarian Project (Campbell & Ramey, 1999) recently found evidence that its graduates at age 21 had higher intelligence-test scores (about a 5-point difference persistently from ages 6½ to 21), higher reading and mathematics achievement test scores, higher educational attainment (35 percent versus 14 percent attending college), less teen pregnancy (average age at first birth 19.1 versus 17.1), and a higher employment rate (65 percent versus 50 percent), but no apparent effect on criminal arrests (Clarke & Campbell, 1998). The Syracuse University Family Development Research Program (Lally, Mangione, & Honig, 1988) found evidence of an effect on juvenile crime as indicated by probation placements (6 percent versus 22 percent). The Elmira Prenatal/Early Infancy Project found the program group reporting fewer arrests than the control group (Olds, Eckenrode, & Henderson, 1997), as well as a variety of positive effects on participating mothers. In addition to the High/Scope and Abecedarian studies, four other studies, including the study of the Early Training Project (Gray, Ramsey, & Klaus, 1982), found evidence of an effect on high school graduation rate (Schweinhart et al., 1993).

The simple conclusion of all of these studies is that early childhood programs that are of high quality can have important short- and long-term effects on children. Such programs *can* have these effects, but every program does not automatically have them. So the question is: What are the characteristics of effective programs that distinguish them from ineffective programs?

WHAT MAKES A GOOD PRESCHOOL PROGRAM

Early childhood program quality has two faces: structural and process. Structural quality consists of stable program characteristics that are specified by administrators and policymakers, such as staff qualifications and staff-child ratio. Those outside the program can specify it, record it, and strongly influence, if not control it. Process quality consists of the behavior of adults and children in the program, such as teacher-child interaction and teacher-parent interaction. It is what happens in the program and is determined entirely by program participants; outsiders must observe the program to detect it. Structural quality affects child outcomes through its effects on process quality. For example, having fewer children per adult (an aspect of structural quality) contributes to children's development if it leads adults to spend more time with individual children (an aspect of process quality).

Schweinhart (1988) identified the following seven elements of the structural quality of early childhood programs:

- A child development curriculum;
- Low enrollment limits;
- Trained staff;
- Supervisory support and inservice training;
- Parent outreach;
- Sensitivity to the non-educational needs of children and families; and
- Developmentally appropriate evaluation procedures.

Each of these seven elements is based on findings of long-term effects from studies previously cited and short-term effects from studies of program quality (e.g., Child Care Cost, Quality and Outcomes Study Team, 1995; Whitebook, Howes, & Phillips, 1989).

A CHILD DEVELOPMENT CURRICULUM

A child development curriculum is based on child-initiated learning activities rather than teacher-directed instruction. The classroom is arranged and the daily routine set up so that young children select and design their own activities during a substantial portion of the day. The teacher's role is to support and facilitate these activities. At other times, the teacher takes charge of group activities, but builds into these activities various opportunities for the children to select and design their own activities.

Long-term evidence for this approach comes from the High/Scope Preschool Curriculum Comparison study (Schweinhart & Weikart, 1997), which examined the effects of three curriculum models on young children living in poverty, two of them based on child-initiated learning activities (High/Scope and Nursery School), the other a model based on fast-paced teacher-directed instruction with lots of reinforcement of children's correct responses (called Direct Instruction). During their school years, only 6 percent of the child-initiated-activities groups required treatment for emotional impairment or disturbance, while this was the case for 47 percent of the Direct Instruction group. By age 23, only 10 percent of the High/Scope group and 17 percent of the Nursery School group had been arrested for a felony at least once, while this was the case for 39 percent of the Direct Instruction group.

To obtain the long-term program effects identified in the High/Scope Perry Preschool Study or some other such study, it is necessary to substantially replicate the program studied, whatever the elements of quality involved. Regarding curriculum, the implication is to use the High/Scope educational approach (Hohmann & Weikart, 1995). The Nursery School approach used in the curriculum study described above also shows promise, but was too broadly defined to permit substantial replication. Surely, other curriculum models could produce long-term effects, but it is difficult to accept claims without evidence.

LOW ENROLLMENT LIMITS

The evidence from various studies associates better outcomes for children with smaller group sizes and fewer children per adults: 16 to 20 three-to five-year-olds with two adults is an effective configuration. These numbers are substantially lower than the norm for U.S. elementary schools, even kindergartens, in part because younger children require more individual attention than older children and in part because early childhood educators in the United States have insisted upon lower numbers of children. These lower numbers strongly support a child development curriculum based on child-initiated activities. Higher numbers pressure teachers toward a teacher-directed approach.

TRAINED STAFF

It is commonly found that teachers with bachelor's degrees in early childhood education or a related discipline have higher-quality classrooms and better child outcomes than do teachers who do not have such degrees. Such marker variables are gross indicators of the amount of relevant training and education, and relevance varies from course to course, even from class session to class session. What is really important is effective training and education in early childhood education that contributes to teachers' ability to deliver process quality in their classrooms.

SUPERVISORY SUPPORT AND INSERVICE TRAINING

Early childhood program supervisors should support teachers and the child development curriculum they use. A first step is for supervisors and teachers to reach a consensus on program goals and emphasis. One of the clearest ways of achieving this consensus and providing supervisory support is to provide opportunities for inservice training on the child development curriculum. One study found that in Head Start, such inservice training was more strongly associated with program quality and effectiveness than were academic degrees (Epstein, 1999), a possibility that can be realized when the inservice training is itself high quality and consistently supportive of program goals.

PARENT OUTREACH

Parent involvement is the goal, but outreach to parents and guardians is the element of program quality needed to reach this goal. Precisely because of the many obstacles to parent involvement that exist today, staff must focus intensely and creatively on ways to get parents involved. Program staff must recognize that they are working in partnership with parents to further their joint contribution to children's development. Staff need to inform parents about the curriculum principles they are using and learn from parents about the unique histories and circumstances of each child. The obvious focus of such communication is the child's progress in the program. Staff can build on a parents' interest in their children learning the ABCs to give them a rich set of ideas about children's emergent literacy and how they can contribute to its development.

SENSITIVITY TO THE NONEDUCATIONAL NEEDS OF CHILDREN AND FAMILIES

Young children come from various family circumstances that affect them educationally and developmentally. They may live in two-parent families, single-parent families, or some other configuration. Their mothers may be employed away from home or not. They may live in poverty or at any other level of the economic spectrum, deeply affecting their living conditions, health, and nutrition. All early childhood programs must be sensitive to these circumstances, but especially those programs that serve children who have special problems—economically disadvantaged, dealing with various types of disabilities, or otherwise at risk of school failure. Policymakers should look at children from all angles in developing programs, but some programs, such as Head Start, dedicate staffing and resources to these problems, and others do not. Whatever their program situation, staff need to be sensitive to all the needs of the children and families they serve.

DEVELOPMENTALLY APPROPRIATE EVALUATION PROCEDURES

Different early childhood programs deal with program evaluation in various ways, but good program evaluation will enhance the professional status of any type of early childhood program and its staff (Schweinhart, 1999). A good evaluation examines program quality and effectiveness, relying largely on systematic observation procedures. Child testing can be appropriate as a supplement to systematic observation of children, but it is critical that such testing be fully consistent with program goals. Too often, child testing is at odds with program goals, leading many to question the value of child testing and even to oppose child assessment in general. But systematic observation overcomes many of the objections to child testing by letting the child take the lead in the activities that are assessed.

These seven elements of quality are structural, set by policymakers and administrators in advance. Now let's look at process quality and how teachers and parents can work together to achieve it.

WORKING TOGETHER TO
GET CHILDREN READY TO SUCCEED

Teachers and parents must first agree that their common goal is to contribute to children's development. The first national education goal is getting children ready to learn in school, and some might view this goal narrowly as teaching children their numbers, letters, shapes, and colors. But the official definition of readiness to learn by the National Education Goals Panel is virtually synonymous with child development, including physical well-being and motor development, social and emotional development, approaches toward learning, language development, and cognition and general knowledge. This position of broad focus on children's development has considerable support.

A second part of this discussion is prioritizing the goal of contributing to children's development versus other early childhood program goals, particularly contributing to family self-sufficiency and taking care of children while parents are otherwise occupied. Contributing to family self-sufficiency is a goal of Head Start programs. It is linked to contributing to children's development to the extent that it includes family child-rearing practices, but it is also independent of this linkage. Taking care of children while parents are otherwise occupied is a goal of child care programs. It is linked to contributing to children's development to the extent that child care equates to early childhood education, but the two goals can conflict with each other if child care is instead considered only a custodial service that does not require professional practitioners.

The program's process quality or practices then flow from the program goals. To have a child development curriculum based on child-initiated activities, the classroom arrangement and daily routine must support these activities. The High/Scope approach accomplishes this by arranging the classroom into interest areas that are delineated by low shelves and other furniture. The daily routine has time for children to plan, do, and review their activities, as well as for cleanup, small-group and large-group activities, and outside times. The teacher supports child-initiated activities throughout the day and particularly during the plan-do-review process. Teachers focus on key experiences in child development that children engage in, rather than behavioral objectives that they require of children.

Parents can apply these same principles as well. They can set aside play areas in their homes and have special places where each toy is put away. When they spend time with children, they can ask them to plan their own activities and support them in carrying out these activities. They too can focus on key experiences in children's development.

Teachers and parents best help children get ready for school when they realize that they are helping them get ready for life. School is not an end in itself, but a means to the ends of educational and economic productivity and social responsibility. The value of learning letters and numbers is realized only when children put those letters and numbers to work for them in reading, writing, and arithmetic, and when they put these skills to work for them in solving life's various challenges and problems. Although reading and writing are important to life in a literate society, speaking, listening, and social skills are probably more important most of the time. As we look to preschool programs to get children ready for school, we should remember the broad definition of child development and school readiness. All our children will be better off for it.

REFERENCES

Barnett, W. S. (1996). *Lives in the balance: The Age-27 benefit-cost analysis of the High/Scope Perry Preschool Program.* Ypsilanti, MI: High/Scope Press.

Berrueta-Clement, J. R., Schweinhart, L. J., Barnett, W. S., Epstein, A. S., & Weikart, D. P. (1984). *Changed lives: The effects of the Perry Preschool Program on youths through age 19.* (Monographs of the High/Scope Educational Research Foundation, No. 8). Ypsilanti, MI: High/Scope Press.

Bloom, B. S. (1964). *Stability and change in human characteristics.* New York: John Wiley & Sons.

Campbell, F. A., & Ramey, C. T. (1999). *Early learning, later success: The Abecedarian Study—Early childhood educational intervention for poor children; Executive summary.* http://www.fpg.unc.edu/~abc/embargoed/executive_summary.htm.

Child Care Cost, Quality, and Child Outcomes Study Team. (1995). *Cost, quality, and child outcomes in child care centers.* Denver: University of Colorado at Denver, Economics Department.

Clarke, S. H., & Campbell, F. A. (1998). Can intervention early prevent crime later? The Abecedarian Project compared with other programs. *Early Childhood Research Quarterly, 13,* 319–344.

Consortium for Longitudinal Studies (1983). *As the twig is bent . . . lasting effects of preschool programs.* Hillsdale, NJ: Erlbaum.

Epstein, A. S. (1999). Pathways to quality in Head Start, public school, and private nonprofit early childhood programs. *Journal of Research in Childhood Education, 13*(2), 101–119.

Gray, S. W., Ramsey, B. K., & Klaus, R. A. (1982). *From 3 to 20: The Early Training Project.* Baltimore, MD: University Park Press.

Hohmann, M., & Weikart, D. P. (1995). *Educating young children: Active learning practices for preschool and child care programs.* Ypsilanti, MI: High/Scope Press.

Hunt, J. M. (1961). *Intelligence and experience.* New York: Ronald Press.

Klaus, R. A., & Gray, S. W. (1968). The Early Training Project for disadvantaged children. *Monographs of the Society for Research in Child Development, 33*(4, Serial No. 120).

Lally, J. R., Mangione, P. L., & Honig, A. S. (1988). The Syracuse University Family Development Research Program: Long-range impact of an early intervention with low-income children and their families. In D. R. Powell (Ed.), *Parent education as early childhood intervention: Emerging directions in theory, research, and practice* (pp. 79–104). Norwood, NJ: Ablex.

McKey, R. H., Condelli, L., Ganson, H., Barrett, B. J., McConkey, C., & Plantz, M. C. (1985). *The impact of Head Start on children, families and communities.* (Final report of the Head Start Evaluation, Synthesis, and Utilization project). Washington, DC: CSR Inc.

Olds, D. L., Eckenrode, J., & Henderson, C. R. Jr., et al. (1997). Long-term effects of home visitation on maternal life course, child abuse and neglect, and children's arrests: Fifteen year follow-up of a randomized trial. *Journal of the American Medical Association, 278*(8), 637–643.

Piaget, J. (1960). *The psychology of intelligence.* Totowa, NJ: Littlefield, Adams.

Schweinhart, L. J. (1988). *A school administrator's guide to early childhood programs.* Ypsilanti, MI: High/Scope Press.

Schweinhart, L. J. (1999, Spring). Evaluating early childhood programs: Key step on the professional path. *High/Scope ReSource.*

Schweinhart, L. J., Barnes, H. V., & Weikart, D. P., with Barnett, W. S., & Epstein, A. S. (1993). *Significant benefits: The High/Scope Perry Preschool study through age 27.* Ypsilanti, MI: High/Scope Press.

Schweinhart, L. J., & Weikart, D. P. (1980). *Young children grow up: The effects of the Perry Preschool Program on youths through age 15.* (Monographs of the High/Scope Educational Research Foundation, No. 7). Ypsilanti, MI: High/Scope Press.

Schweinhart, L. J., & Weikart, D. P. (1997). *Lasting differences: The High/Scope Preschool Curriculum Comparison Study through age 23.* Ypsilanti, MI: High/Scope Press.

Weikart, D. P., Bond, J. T., & McNeil, J. T. (1978). *The Ypsilanti Perry Preschool Project: Preschool years and longitudinal results through fourth grade.* Ypsilanti, MI: High/Scope Press.

Weikart, D. P., Deloria, D. J., Lawser, S. A., & Wiegerink, R. (1970). *Longitudinal results of the Ypsilanti Perry Preschool Project.* Ypsilanti, MI: High/Scope Press.

Weikart, D. P., Epstein, A. S., Schweinhart, L. J., & Bond, J. T. (1978). *The Ypsilanti Preschool Curriculum Demonstration Project: Preschool years and longitudinal results.* Ypsilanti, MI: High/Scope Press.

Westinghouse Learning Corporation. (1969). *The impact of Head Start: An evaluation of the effects of Head Start on children's cognitive and affective development* (Vols. 1 and 2). Washington, DC: Clearinghouse for Federal, Scientific, and Technical Information.

Whitebook, M., Howes, C., & Phillips, D. (1989). *Who cares? Child care teachers and the quality of care in America.* Oakland, CA: Child Care Employee Project.

"Every Child Will Succeed— No Excuses!" The 1,000 Days to Success School Network

Stephen Kay and Craig Wheaton

There's a new watchword on the front lines of school reform. It is "1,000 Days." This watchword defines a growing network of schools committed to ensuring 100-percent literacy in elementary schools. Every school in the network promises, in writing, that every child entering kindergarten will learn to read by the end of 2nd grade—no excuses. (See the appendix to this chapter for the method of calculating the 1,000 days.)

Each school spells out its commitment on a printed warranty card, with warranty terms displayed prominently on the back. This "fine print" details the responsibilities that the school, teachers, and parents must fulfill to avoid nullifying the warranty.

Seems simple enough. After all, isn't that what schools are supposed to do—teach kids to read? Reading is the first step toward success. Yet the 1,000 Days to Success School Network is reaching for 100-percent literacy, a goal never achieved before.

In the minds of the network's pioneers, it's more than a goal. It's a force of history whose moment has come. It is time for teachers, parents, and administrators to ensure early learning success for every child—no excuses.

How It Began

The founder of 1,000 Days, Steve Kay, principal of Scott Lane Elementary School in Santa Clara, California, recalls when the idea first dawned on him:

One morning in April 1997 I heard the radio DJ announce that there were only a thousand days left in the century. It struck me that our incoming kindergarten students would also have only a thousand days between the time they entered Scott Lane and their "graduation" from 2nd grade in June 2000. What was the most important thing we could do for those children in that time period? Teach them to read!

That same week, I happened to buy a new set of tires for my car. The transaction included a review of the tire warranty. By the time the salesman and I had finished reviewing the fine print, I realized that the tire manufacturer was not the only party responsible for my tires. As the owner, I had to rotate them regularly, I had to keep them properly inflated, and I'd better not drive them over nails!

All of a sudden, in my mind's eye, I saw Scott Lane's little kindergarteners and all the "nails" along their path to reading success. I combined the two images—the tire warranty and the urgency of the 1,000 days—into the "Reading Warranty" program, which I proposed to my staff. Their response? For the first time in my career as a principal, I received a standing ovation. Challenged and inspired by the warranty metaphor, my staff unanimously committed to guarantee literacy for 100 percent of our students.

Throughout the fall of 1997, the staff worked together to define the terms of the warranty and inform the parents of 115 kindergarteners about this new, serious commitment to their children's success in reading (Sagor, 2000). In November the commitment became more public when *The San Jose Mercury News* (Suryaraman, 1997) ran a front-page story about the program at Scott Lane Elementary School.

NETWORKING TO REDEFINE LITERACY

In the spring of 1998, the four California schools described below joined together to establish the 1,000 Days to Success School Network.

• Scott Lane Elementary, in the heart of Silicon Valley, has students speaking 22 different languages. Nearly 70 percent qualify for free or reduced lunch.

• Bret Harte and John C. Fremont Schools are located in Corcoran, California, at the center of the San Joaquin Valley. Corcoran's demographics are similar to many rural farming communities: nearly 50 percent are English language learners, 82 percent qualify for free or reduced-cost lunch, and 37 percent are in the Federal Migrant Education program.

• Center Street School wedges itself between the Los Angeles airport, an oil refinery, and a major Interstate highway. Minorities make up 35 percent of its 1,200 students with 12 percent qualifying for free and reduced-cost lunch.

Many children come to these schools not knowing how to hold a book, never having been read to. Many of these obstacles to learning have been used as excuses for failure. But network school educators are not satisfied with excuses; our schools are committed to success.

At the same time that the network schools made the commitment to early literacy, there was a tidal wave of change on the horizon. Test scores showed that California students were near the bottom in reading. In response, the state mandated reduced class sizes, and the California Reading Initiative provided funds for teacher retraining.

Faced with this tidal wave of change, our schools had two choices: drown or, to use a California metaphor, grab a board and surf the wave. The 1,000 Days to Success Network schools have chosen to jump on the reading warranty "surfboard." So far, the ride has been both exhilarating and exhausting, not only a reinforcement of why we all chose education as a career but also, to be honest, a test of our stamina and nerves.

INSTRUCTION DRIVEN BY EARLY RESULTS

The teaching profession faces a mammoth challenge, as 40 percent of 4th graders nationwide are not reading at grade level. Increasingly, only one fate awaits most children who do not learn to read—failure. Politicians blame educators, and everyone demands results. The public is tired of excuses. At 1,000 Days schools, we embrace accountability. We track and report student progress in short intervals, and we keep parents and the community informed.

Administrators and teachers discuss effective instruction and intervention based on regularly collected data. Teachers collect data, make adjustments in teaching, measure results, make readjustments, and again measure results. While collecting student data, teachers also document successful instructional strategies and add them to a locally developed knowledge base for teaching. And as teachers increasingly take charge of quality control, they also feel more empowered to improve student learning (Schmoker, 1996).

Assessing what a child does know is the foundation for improvement. Teachers know each child's success level and work toward established quarterly benchmarks of progress. Network schools have adopted a Language

Observation Survey (LOS) that provides administrators, teachers, and parents ongoing measures of progress. Adapted from Reading Recovery founder Marie Clay's work, the LOS includes assessments of letter identification, concepts about print, and "leveled text" mastery (Clay, 1993).

PARTNERSHIP FOR SUCCESS

As shown in Figure 13.1, 1,000 Days to Success is a partnership between the school, its teachers and support staff, the community, students, and parents. Through teamwork and commitment to a common goal, everyone has a role in a child's success.

The entire school community supports the child with specific actions in a coordinated effort that embodies the old African proverb, "It takes a village to raise a child." Network schools are working to "create the village" to raise its children.

Our village involves partnerships among the school, teachers, parents-to-classroom, parents-to-parents, community, and businesses. We ask that learning obstacles be overcome in these partnerships so that every child has a chance to succeed.

"The main thing is to keep the main thing, the main thing!" (Jim Barksdale as quoted in Labovitz & Rosansky, 1997). Staffs at the network schools repeat this quote almost like a mantra, adding: "And literacy is the main thing!" All schools have implemented an uninterrupted morning time block devoted to literacy—no assemblies, no announcements over the P.A. system—just literacy experiences tailored to meet the needs of every child.

Teachers focus on maximizing instructional time. Time efficiency is a critical factor in school improvement (Allington & Cunningham, 1995). We calculated reading instructional time and found that teachers had only 30 minutes a week of direct literacy instruction with each student! (See the appendix to this chapter for the breakdown and calculation of direct instruction time.) The urgency of the 1,000 Days countdown became a great motivator!

The network is devoted to supporting schools as they build capacity. For example, a key staff position is the on-site literacy coordinator. When teachers need assistance, the literacy coordinator is available to model strategies in the classroom and to help in whatever ways are needed. We refer to the literacy coordinator's activities as "just-in-time" staff development, as opposed to the traditional one-day "drive-by."

The need to reach every student has changed the atmosphere of the traditional student-study team. In the past, in order to help a child who was

FIGURE 13.1
THE LEARNING "VILLAGE"

not making adequate academic progress, a team comprising the child's teacher, a resource specialist, the principal, and occasionally the child's parents met monthly. Today, because teachers feel the urgency to succeed, many network schools have found it necessary to have study-team meetings every week. The team meetings focus heavily on parental involvement. The team often recommends family counseling or parenting classes. The team's focus is on early intervention to address learning disabilities, poor attendance patterns, vision and hearing problems, and other obstacles to learning.

Schools are using cross-age tutors to help improve reading. In Corcoran, California, high school students, who have been trained in early reading intervention strategies, tutor 1st-grade students. At Scott Lane, upper elementary students are trained to work with 1st- and 2nd-graders in reading. Both programs are examples of how a school system can use existing resources (even students) to promote early success in reading.

One simple strategy that has had tremendous positive effect is to know each child's instructional level and to provide instructional strategies, materials, and time at that level. This has been a difficult adjustment for many teachers; so often we try to fit the child into an arbitrary grade-level curriculum. Our strategy is not about working students harder, but working them smarter.

The administration and school provide the support staff, facilities, and structure to support 1,000 Days to Success. Resources, staff development specialists, instructional assistants, office staff, and other support services are all directed toward supporting every child's success.

TEACHERS

There are no "silver bullets." The "reading wars" are meaningless and get in the way of doing what needs to be done. Each teacher understands that a *program* is not going to teach a child to read; it will take the professional skill of a classroom teacher.

We have not found one curriculum or program that magically teaches every child to read. Our approach is to employ every available resource that demonstrates potential usefulness. We use all the weapons in our pedagogical arsenal—and continually look for better ones—to win the battle against illiteracy.

Many of our instructional techniques and strategies have evolved out of a number of early literacy learning initiatives such as Ohio State University's Literacy Collaborative and California Early Literacy Learning (CELL) (National Research Council, 1998; California State Board of Education, 1999). As many as 20 percent of our students actually have one-on-one intervention from teachers trained in Reading Recovery.

Research is documenting the conclusion that without sustained staff development for teachers and ongoing reinforcement activities for students, many students do not maintain the gains they made during pull-out, support programs. The key is to build robust classroom environments with effective teaching and learning techniques and strategies that work as a safety net for all children (National Research Council, 1998). We continue to use every effective weapon in our war against illiteracy.

Teachers pledge to practice open communication with parents, initiating frequent meetings and maintaining an ongoing relationship. Parents are welcomed in the classroom and invited to help. They are informed about the literacy program, provided weekly reports, and respected as a full partner in our endeavor.

PARENTS-TO-CLASSROOM PARTNERSHIP

Open communication is a two-way street. Parents are encouraged to read and return notes and phone calls from teachers. Teachers model effective communication as they develop an ongoing relationship with each parent.

At the core of the parent's role is to provide a home structure that will enhance learning. Children are at school only 540 of the 1,000 days between kindergarten and the end of 2nd grade. Thus, home routines that support literacy are powerful learning opportunities. Parents are asked to read with their child at least 10 minutes every day and to provide consistent homework support. Training, modeling, and reminders help parents in this effort.

Using the tire warranty metaphor, children need to be kept inflated and protected from running over nails, curbs, bumps, and rough roads. This protection involves regular health, vision, hearing, and dental checkups and a nurturing home environment in which television time is monitored.

In addition to sending children to school ready to learn—dressed, clean, fed, well-rested, loved, and healthy—parents are asked to help in and out of the classroom. Most importantly, children cannot learn if they are not in school. We do confront early learning problems honestly, directly, and positively. We know that not every child is going to arrive at school with all the above factors, but we don't give up on any child. We do everything possible to solve problems early in the child's school experience.

PARENTS-TO-PARENTS PARTNERSHIP

Many of our parents need help and training in order to be good parents. Every parent wants his or her child to succeed, but many do not have the skills to provide the environment necessary for success. Parent education and training is an area we are continuing to improve. We don't give up on a child because of the lack of skill or responsibility of the parent. To build the capacity of parents, network schools are establishing parent training, reading programs, parenting classes, and English language training. Many social agencies are coordinating their services with us.

The Parent Teacher Association, School Site Council, and advisory committees give parents a voice in the schools. Evening programs for families are focused on specific topics and designed to provide materials, training, and ideas for family activities in math, science, literacy, behavior management, motor-skill development, and language development.

COMMUNITY

While the school staff, teachers, and parents are key members of the "learning village," community members and businesses also must do their part. For example, each of our schools has instituted volunteer reading programs. Hitachi Data Systems employees spend 25 hours per week as volunteers in an adopt-a-kid-to-read program at Scott Lane. The El Segundo

Middle School students who take a Peer Assistance Class learn how to teach students to read. Two times per week the Middle School students visit Center Street Elementary School to work with selected students in 2nd grade. Business leaders from Corcoran's local Rotary club visit Fremont School to read to classes every other Friday.

BUSINESS/INDUSTRY

Additionally, many of our schools have had significant financial support from business and community partners. Hitachi Data Systems, Chevron Oil, Computer Science Corporation, Lithographix Inc., and Mead Paper have contributed to their local schools by developing and printing school brochures.

Scott Lane School has developed a partnership with the Waterford Early Literacy program. Through this partnership students are supported with rich technology. Plans are now developing to expand the use of the Waterford system throughout the network.

Lemoore Naval Air Station donated nearly 100 computers to support the Accelerated Reader program at John C. Fremont School.

RESULTS

Scott Lane School in the Santa Clara Unified School District celebrated its 1000th day in June 2000. the front page headline in the San Jose Mercury News proclaimed, "Pledge spells victory for students' reading." The story continued, "Against all odds, all but four of the 60 second-graders still remaining on campus from the original kindergarten class met the school's reading standard" (Suryaraman, 2000). Ninety-five percent of the first graduating class—kindergarten to second grade—was reading at grade level or above. Even more significant, this class scored 14 percentile points higher than the prior class on the statewide reading portion of the Stanford Achievement Test (SAT9).

In Corcoran, the first group of 1000 Days students finished first grade. Efforts were paying off. More than 75 percent of the warranty class was reading at grade level. The second graders improved 9 percentile points on the reading, 7 percentile on language, and 7 percentile on mathematics on the SAT9 over the last year's second grade.

Center Street School had nearly 100 percent of their warranty students reading at or above grade level after the spring assessments at the end of the students' second year in the 1000 Days program.

Perhaps the most significant results are the intensive efforts made for those who need extra help. In the past, students were sent on to the next grade level with a hope and a prayer. Now, individual plans are being implemented to follow students into special summer programs, before- and after-school programs, and beyond—to the next grade-level teacher.

1,000 DAYS TO REFORM

At the start of the program, we saw the 1,000 Days time line in terms of a deadline for 100-percent literacy. As we continued the commitment to making all of our students better readers, we found the reform spreading throughout other aspects of our schools as well. It is not just about early literacy; it is about school reform (Schlechty, 1997).

As we began the process of doing whatever it takes to ensure that our students would become readers, we found that we were also reforming our schools from the ground up. Our schools began the 1,000 Days journey with the first guaranteed class. Though we have made changes at all levels, we focused on building capacity in our system as the first class progresses from kindergarten to 2nd grade. This process is "doable," but the pressure builds each year. Doing "whatever it takes" became the mantra of every teacher and the promise to every student. It became the heart of the school culture.

RESULTS-BASED MANAGEMENT

The era of accountability undermines efforts to involve all stakeholders in decision making. Some administrators and policy makers have recently called school-based management into question. But effective reform must involve everyone; what matters cannot be mandated (Fullan, 1993). Network schools are instituting a new era of school-based management based on results. Results-based management is a practical blend of accountability and collaborative participation in school decision making.

Past attempts to implement school-based management failed because of "time" issues. Schools did not drastically alter the structure of the day, and without fundamental restructuring, there is not enough time for widespread involvement. The 1,000 Days Network is using advanced communication tools to bridge the time gap. Results-based management is made possible by providing input through virtual, asynchronous committee meetings.

The 1,000 Days Web site provides schools with electronic discussion space. Teachers can participate in committees, providing input and leadership without actually having to attend meetings. All staff members can keep up with all committees by reading postings of committee minutes, and they can reply with input and reactions. This committee structure is available on the Web and is accessible any time on a password-protected site (http://www.1000-days.org). This e-leadership management approach includes the use of e-mail, e-discussions, and online meetings.

A JOURNEY WORTH JOINING

On the surface, the mission of the 1,000 Days to Success School Network seems almost pedestrian. Teaching reading is, after all, no more than what schools are supposed to do. The reality, of course, is quite different, and the goal is hardly just a minor fix. We are focusing our efforts on making sure every child learns to read—*no excuses*. We know the challenges that we face with our students; we see it in their eyes. We've also seen the sparkle in the eyes of students who, upon finishing a good book, proudly announce: "I can read!" Every child deserves that chance to succeed. Schools must join together to share successful practices, staff development models, and resources to create that environment where success is the norm for every child.

REFERENCES

Allington, R. L., & Cunningham, P. M. (1995). *Schools that work: Where all children read and write.* Reading, MA: Addison-Wesley.

California State Board of Education (Ed.). (1999). *Read all about it! Readings to inform the profession.* Sacramento, CA: Author.

Clay, M. M. (1993). *An observation survey of early literacy achievement.* Portsmouth, NH: Heinemann.

Fullan, M. (1993). *Change forces: Probing the depths of educational reform.* Bristol, CT: The Falmer Press.

Labovitz, G., & Rosansky, V. (1997). *The power of alignment: How great companies stay centered and accomplish extraordinary things.* New York: John Wiley and Sons.

National Research Council. (1998). *Preventing reading difficulties in young children.* Washington, DC: National Research Council.

Sagor, R. (2000). *Guiding school improvement with action research.* Alexandria, VA: Association for Supervision and Curriculum Development.

Schlechty, P. C. (1997). *Inventing better schools: An action plan for educational reform.* San Francisco: Jossey-Bass.

Schmoker, M. (1996). *Results: The key to continuous school improvement.* Alexandria, VA: Association for Supervision and Curriculum Development.

Suryaraman, M. (1997, November 30). Reading "warranty cards" for kindergartners. *The San Jose Mercury News,* p. A1.

Suryaraman, M. (2000, June 12). Pledge spells victory for students' reading. *The San Jose Mercury News,* p. A1.

APPENDIX: 1,000 DAYS TO SUCCESS

1,000 days (3 years)	Calendar days from kindergarten to "graduation" from 2nd grade
180 days × 3 years = 540 days	Children are actually in school only 180 days a year; 180 × 3 = 540 school days
540 days × 2-hour block = 1,080 hours	540 days times 2 hours per day equals total 1,080 hours of literacy instruction in 3 years
1,080 hours ÷ 4 guided reading groups = 270 hours per reading group	We expect each teacher to have a guided reading lesson with each student each day. In the 2-hour block, each teacher meets with one reading group every half-hour. Divide the 1,080 hours that students are working directly on literacy by the 4 groups of students that are actually working with their teacher; this equals 270 hours for each reading group
270 hours ÷ 5 students = 54 hours per student	Divide the 270 hours each guided reading group is with the teacher by the 5 students in the group, and a student gets the individual attention of the teacher only 54 hours
54 hours ÷ 3 years = 18 hours per year	The 54 hours is spread over 3 years. Divide the 54 hours by 3 years; there are only 18 hours of direct instruction per year
18 hours ÷ 36 weeks = ½ hour per week	There are 36 weeks in an average school year. Divide the 18 hours by the number of weeks, and you see that a student may have only 30 minutes per week of individual instruction during the entire 1,000 days

TEACHING TO ALL OF A CHILD'S INTELLIGENCES

Peter Kline

I believe that education begins as a process that closely resembles artistic and scientific discovery. Observe a child at play in the nursery, and you will witness the creative process transparently revealed in what happens there. If you videotape a half-hour or so of some child at play, you'll be able to notice in repeated viewing the same creative process that emerges as a painter works on a canvas, a physicist on a Theory of Everything, or a biologist in search of a new way of understanding ecology. What you'll see is the nonlinear exploration of a variety of recurring themes, spiraling gradually toward insights that will forever change behavior. (These ideas are explored more fully in my book *The Everyday Genius* [1988] and in the videotape of a child at play derived from a program done for PBS in the "Author, Author" series.)

Exploring an unfamiliar object, the child will confront it with every aspect of self. Tongue, hands, feet, eyes, ears, and solar plexus will all get wrapped around it. Time and again the child will have an "ah-ha" experience, a Gestalt formation, that says something like, "This door knob is the kind of object that enables me to open all doors." Such insights are gained only through repeated exploration and experience.

Language itself is created in this way, for we all invent our own unique forms of expression. The best book on language from this point of view is *The Language Instinct* (Pinker, 1994). No two people have exactly the same vocabulary, and throughout our childhood, we add six to twelve new words of our own selection to our personal glossary every day.

Teachers can learn to take advantage of this completely natural way of learning much more actively than they do now. Most of our models of teaching are rooted in the model that developed a thousand years ago when books were extremely rare, so the only way to pass on the information in them was for those who had read a few books to lecture to those who couldn't get access to them.

Today teachers sometimes stand in front of the room and tell their students both the concepts they should understand and how to develop certain skills. For a few of the students, who are primarily logical, linguistic, and auditory in the way they learn, this is an effective way of teaching. These students love to hear the teacher talk and, if they get a chance, love to ask questions about what they have heard. Most of the other students, however, have difficulty with this process.

Lecturing is still a valuable way of communicating information, but there are also many other ways. We now know that if you teach in all those other ways, as well as telling the students what they should know or how to do what you want them to do, you should be able to teach all of your students with equal success.

Neuroscientist Howard Gardner has demonstrated that not one or two, but nine different kinds of intelligence work in our brains— differently for each of us. Schools that teach to all nine of these intelligences can, indeed, keep the creativity of early childhood alive in children, while teaching them more than twice as much material twice as effectively in any given period of time now considered normal or standard for the curriculum (Campbell, Campbell, & Dickinson, 1998; Gardner, 1983, 1991, 1999).

Gardner demonstrated that schools as we have known them have treated us as if we had only two intelligences—verbal/linguistic and logical/mathematical—when, in fact, we have seven more: visual/spatial, musical/rhythmic, body/kinesthetic, interpersonal, intrapersonal, existentialist, and naturalist. Each of us has all nine of these, but we configure them in different ways, with some of us leading with only one and some with a combination of several.

Teachers can learn methods that blend the nine intelligences into various combinations. Let me demonstrate this with simple arithmetic.

All children who enter a 1st-grade classroom already know something about arithmetic, but they don't know that they know it. In fact, one of the most common problems with traditional education is that it almost never teaches us how to recognize what we already know.

So here's how to do that with arithmetic:

The teacher has two identical teddy bears or Beanie Babies sitting in front of her in the classroom. She holds up a picture of the top of a piece of cake and shows it to the class. (Here she is appealing to the visual, or spatial, intelligence.) Then she says, "I am going to cut this cake and share it between my two children." (This act of sharing appeals to the interpersonal intelligence, in that it's a social interaction.)

She then cuts the cake into two very unequal pieces, giving one to one of her "children" and one to the other.

Then she asks the class, "How many thought that was fair?" (Invoking the idea of fairness in this way appeals to the existential intelligence, as the child's basic philosophical judgments about fairness are invoked.)

We can hope that no hands will go up.

She then asks her students to tell her why they didn't think it was fair.

After several explanations, she takes another drawing of the cake and asks, "Do you want me to cut this into two equal parts?" (This invokes the logical/mathematical intelligence: "Here's the problem, now let's consider the solution.")

She then shows the cake in its two parts to the class and brings them together. "This is one half of the cake, and this is the other. When I bring them together, I have a whole cake. It's true that I didn't put the cake back together, but still I have all of it there, don't I?"

(Note that some children will not believe you have a whole cake once you have cut it in half. You have to begin teaching children that numbers describe amount but not state. In other words, numbers can tell you how much cake there is, but nothing about whether or not it is split down the middle. This is an abstraction, and no one can really understand how this kind of abstraction works. The best way to teach the concept of abstraction is to show many different examples like the cake and discuss which aspects of the object numbers can describe and which aspects numbers cannot describe.)

Next the teacher invites two children to come to the front of the room and stand shoulder to shoulder. (This is primarily body/kinesthetic, but it is also interpersonal, as the children—both those doing and those watching—are thinking about the people involved and seeing a connection between the mathematical and social interactions. It is also intrapersonal, because it enables one to identify personally with the concept of one-half.)

"We're going to pretend that when Billy and Susie stand together like this, they stand for a birthday cake. Now we're going to cut the cake in half. Billy and Susie, will you move away from each other?" (This is now also emphasizing the visual/spatial intelligence.)

Billy and Susie move apart.

"See? Now we have cut the cake in half. Now we're going to bring Billy and Susie together again." Billy and Susie stand together again. "Now, once again the whole cake is in place. Billy, come here and stand by me." Billy does so. "Now I have half the cake. I have left the other half of the cake on the table."

The teacher writes ½ on the board. "This is the way of writing one-half. Another way of saying this is 'one over two' or 'one divided by two.' When I divided the cake into two parts, I gave each part to one of my children over here. I divided one cake between two children, so each of my children had half of a cake." (Here the previous material is being translated into a linguistic format, by giving the words to describe what has been observed.)

Thus, in a short time, the teacher has taught the children something about the following concepts:

- Fairness.
- The difference between the cake in the abstract as something having mathematical properties and a real cake that you can eat.
- What equality is and how it relates to our natural desire to be fair with each other.
- A representation of division.
- A representation of fractions.
- How the word "half" can be represented by numbers.
- How subtraction and addition work (take one away or add one to the other).
- The basis for seeing a relationship between subtraction and division.

None of the children in the class will be consciously aware that they are learning about all these things, but they are learning about them in much the same way that they learned their native language. In other words, you can learn a great deal without even being conscious that you are learning at all.

Children's play is experienced as fun, but it is actually a powerful form of learning. In describing this arithmetic lesson, I am describing a process that looks very much like children's play.

A teacher can dramatize all the different things that must be taught in such a way that they are not only fun to learn but also experienced so that many of the interrelationships between them become clear.

This arithmetic lesson may be extended by having the children work in groups and do arithmetic problems by sorting themselves into various patterns. For example, six children come to the front of the room. You ask them to sort themselves into two groups of three each. You then say, "See, I have divided you into groups of three each. So six divided by two is three." (Here a more systematic view of what is happening emerges, and the focus is now on the naturalist intelligence.)

You then write the problem on the board. You haven't taught them addition yet, but you are already teaching them division. By teaching to all of a child's intelligences, you can help your students understand the deep structure of what they are learning.

Let's look at another example. Everyone should know about the number line and the fact that as you move from left to right on it, you are moving from negative to positive. If zero is placed in the middle, you move from negative numbers to positive numbers. Many of your students will not understand the number line until they have actually walked through it.

Here's one of a zillion ways you have children do that.

Jane stands on the position "minus 10." She says, "When I do this, I owe Tameka 10 cents." She then walks to the "plus 10" position and says, "Now Tameka owes me 10 cents."

Carlos is next. He says, "When I stand here, it is 10 below zero. When I move over here it is 10 above. That's still cold, so I'm going to move here, where it is 70 above."

Then Kwang stands on the position "minus 10" and says, "In this position, it is 10 days before New Year's." He moves to zero and says, "Now it is New Year's." He moves to positive 10 and says, "Now New Year's has been over for 10 days, and I can't wait for my birthday."

Until children have a clear understanding that these different ways of using the number line work the same way but have different implications in real life, they cannot possibly learn to think mathematically.

If your students didn't learn all this in 1st grade, you can still get them to learn it in 6th grade. This kind of teaching can be accomplished at any stage of life.

In the exercise in which the children act out or represent pieces of a math problem, they have used their logical/mathematical intelligence by explaining and discussing the logic of what they are doing. We have appealed to the verbal/linguistic intelligence by translating numbers into common parlance, so that we are teaching using word problems from the beginning. We have invoked their interpersonal intelligence by having children do math together as a social process. Whenever we get into discussions of how we should order things so as to impact our lives for the better—fairness is just one example—we invoke the existential intelligence. We have taught to the intrapersonal intelligence by teaching that math has to do with personal attitudes and values concerning fairness, that you can experience being a number yourself and know what it is like to be part of an arithmetic problem, and that you can personally have fun doing this. To move this activity into the domain of the musical/rhythmic intelligence, have the children write a song about the activity. All that we have done, of course, is kinesthetic, so it is teaching in terms of the body/kinesthetic intelligence. And, of course, it is all visual/spatial as well. Finally, the naturalist intelligence is developed as we learn to notice patterns in what is happening around us. The transformations the teacher performs by having the children move into various groupings is similar to processes that you can observe in nature, like the flight patterns of birds. At no time have we separated activities into one intelligence or another. They are all taught together as a system, exactly the way they work in our day-to-day thinking.

You can teach any concept in any subject this way and, in the process, make it so clear and simple that it will never be forgotten. Once a process is learned in simple terms, the learner can then take it to much higher levels of complexity very quickly.

REFERENCES

Campbell, B., Campbell, L., & Dickinson, D. (1998). *Teaching and learning through multiple intelligences.* Needham Heights, MA: Allyn and Bacon.

Gardner, H. (1983). *Frames of mind: The theory of multiple intelligences.* New York: Basic Books.

Gardner, H. (1991). *The unschooled mind.* New York: Basic Books.

Gardner, H. (1999). *Intelligence reframed: Multiple intelligences for the 21st century.* New York: Basic Books.

Kline, P. (1988). *The everyday genius.* Arlington, VA: Great Ocean.

Pinker, S. (1994). *The language instinct.* New York: William Morrow.

SUGGESTED READING

Armstrong, T. (1987). *In their own way.* Los Angeles: Tarcher.

Botkin, J. W., Elmandjra, M., & Malitza, M. (1979). *No limits to learning: Bridging the human gap (a report to the Club of Rome).* New York: Pergamon.

Buzan, T. (1983). *Use both sides of your brain.* New York: Dutton.

Conroy, P. (1972). *The water is wide.* New York: Bantam Books.

de Bono, E. (1973). *Lateral thinking.* New York: Harper.

Hart, L. (1975). *How the brain works.* New York: Basic Books.

Hart, L. (1983). *Human brain, human learning.* New York: Longman.

Kline, P., & Martel, L. (1992). *School success, the inside story.* Arlington, VA: Great Ocean.

Paulos, J. A. (1991). *Beyond numeracy: Ruminations of a numbers man.* New York: Knopf.

Pearce, J. C. (1977). *Magical child.* New York: Bantam Books.

Pearce, J. C. (1992). *Evolution's end, claiming the potential of our intelligence.* San Francisco: Harper.

Rosenthal, R., & Jacobson, L. (1968). *Pygmalion in the classroom.* New York: Holt, Rinehart and Winston.

Slavin, R. E. (1982). *Cooperative learning.* Washington, DC: National Education Association.

PROJECT FIRST STEP: THE CONNECTION BETWEEN FUNDAMENTAL PHYSICAL SKILLS AND ACADEMIC LEARNING

Thomas R. Johnson

Psychologists have been saying since 1700 that all we know comes through the senses. Neurologists have been saying for 50 years that human beings learn through movement. Yet at age six, the child is placed in a three-foot cubicle and expected to learn.

—Steele, 1976, p. 1

Many children today do not exhibit the physical, emotional, and social readiness skills necessary for successful academic learning. Traditional teaching and classroom management methods may have been successful in the past, when children were more physically active, but the admonition to "sit still, be quiet, and work independently" doesn't seem to be as effective today as it once was.

When the majority of children worked on the farm, did chores around the house, and played outside with neighborhood friends, they were physically preparing to learn. According to research data, children begin to experience and enhance their physical senses in the womb, where they first are able to hear, see, feel, and move (Schurr, 1975). After birth, they begin to explore, discovering fingers, toes, sounds, smells, shapes, and colors. The world is a playground, an adventure, and a classroom, but as children full of wonder grow older, society begins to shrink their world of experience. Children must learn to change everything their senses have been telling them about learning and "playing by the rules."

Many children spend more time in front of the television or playing video games than they do in physically active playing, particularly in homes where there is only one parent, or where both parents work (Schroeder, 1992; Kotulak, 1997; Jensen, 1998). Further, many children now have shorter attention spans due to such factors as the pace of video games and the quick editing of television shows. Considering that major problems are now discovered, related, and solved in 60-minute television shows with commercials included, it's no wonder that many children are impatient with puzzles or lengthy books.

Modern technology has made life easier, but it has also stunted the development of certain basic skills that we used to take for granted. Computers and calculators perform logical and critical thinking for us. Thanks to microwaves and fast foods, we spend less time in kitchens, thereby limiting the development of such skills as exact measuring and stirring, and of such tactile processes as peeling potatoes and kneading bread. Even the modern materials used in clothing can narrow the experience of the senses: for instance, children who wear water-repellent microfiber coats and gloves may rarely smell wet wool or feel it on their bodies.

Today's mobile society has reduced contact with extended family; parents and grandparents may live thousands of miles away from their loved ones. Individual activities outside the home routinely keep family members apart, scheduling incompatibilities limit the shortest excursions together, and families no longer spend the time they used to discussing events of the day over dinner. Many children today do not have the same gross-motor, language, socialization, visual-motor, and visualization experiences as children in previous generations (Winn, 1985; Levin, 1998).

We can define learning problems in different ways. Roach and Kephart have characterized the " 'slow learner' or 'non-achiever' . . . as the child who does not seem to learn academic material from conventional teaching practices" (1966, p. 2). For many of these slow learners, the mind and body are not ready to process the required instruction.

According to Hedges and Hardin (1972), "readiness for learning is not a state that comes to all children automatically; rather the state must be attained. For the child to attain readiness and to be successful with learning, a number of skills and abilities must be developed" (p. 249).

Since the inception of Project First Step (PFS) in 1991, more than 50,000 children have participated in the program activities, and more than 5,000 teachers and staff members in China, Canada, and six U.S. states have been trained in PFS theory and techniques.

Project First Step began in the spring of 1991 as a pull-out program in Union City Elementary School, Union City, Michigan. The state of Michigan provided development funding for the project, while the W. K. Kellogg Foundation invested in its implementation over a three-year period. Though the program was showing dramatic results in its initial format, it soon became apparent that other school districts would not be able to afford to implement it in the same way: a school would have to hire a full-time specialist trained in PFS theory, techniques, and activities, as well as maintaining a room designated for PFS use only.

Lt. Governor Connie Binsfeld observed the program at Union City and suggested that it might fit into the guidelines of the "4, but not yet 5" program instituted throughout the state for "at-risk" children. Project First Step soon began to help students, teachers, and families in the Union City, Marshall, and Olivet school districts. Shortly thereafter, Senator John J. H. Schwarz encouraged the state legislature to include PFS in the Michigan education budget for use in several early childhood education programs.

In the fall of 1993, PFS began a "teacher-training" model at St. Monica School in Kalamazoo, Michigan. This model allowed PFS staff to train teachers and parents through a series of workshops, newsletters, and monthly classroom visits by PFS staff, and was affordable, since existing personnel could be trained in PFS. The format was so successful that schools in five other states have since implemented the program.

Project First Step established yet another training format in the spring of 1997 at Neigebaur Early Childhood Center in Warren, Michigan, and at two schools in the Frankfort School District in Frankfort, Illinois. In this type of training, teachers, volunteers, and parents participate in intense workshops designed to focus their attention on the theory, techniques, activities, and equipment that make the program work. They are provided with all PFS literature, including monthly newsletters for parents that describe the training the teachers and staff are receiving. Teachers actually receive more contact hours in this format than in any other. The format has been well received in these districts and in other schools added this year.

There are three distinct PFS training formats. The first format costs approximately $50,000 and provides the school with a full-time specialist and access to training and facilities. The second format, at around $15,000, provides for monthly visits from a PFS specialist, short workshops, and all material templates. The final and thus far most successful format costs between $7,500 and $10,000 and provides four intensive workshops for the entire staff, one all-day screening seminar workshop, and all material templates.

While most school districts are concerned about the increasing numbers of learning-disabled students and "at-risk" students, those that have used PFS techniques have

- reduced the learning disabled population,
- raised student self-esteem,
- regularized "at-risk" student attendance,
- discovered that children are better prepared to learn, and
- detected a pattern of better academic and social learning.

Most impressively, schools continue to implement PFS wherever training has taken place, and teachers and parents appear to value its theory and techniques.

The following are the key concepts for student learning under the program:

• **Children need the ability to remain on task.** Project First Step helps children develop physical skills that improve their ability to focus on a task until it is completed. For instance, children work on developing movement skills, such as balance, which require tremendous concentration.

• **Children need to be able to track while reading.** Eyes are controlled by sets of muscles that operate in tandem. When under stress, as they are in reading, these muscles sometimes have trouble working together. Because muscle control is a physiological skill, it can be developed through movement activities prescribed by PFS, such as bouncing a balloon in the air and watching it rise and fall. The speed at which a balloon bobs up and down allows eyes to gradually begin working in conjunction as they follow the object.

• **Children need to know how to get from point A to point B.** As students attempt to solve more and more difficult assignments, such as story problems in mathematics, or to follow more difficult story lines in reading, they must learn how to sequence events. Through step-by-step sequencing of physical tasks, children learn to follow steps in order to reach an end result.

• **Children need to know how to follow directions.** A person cannot survive in the world without learning to follow directions. By teaching children to obey the word "no" in infancy, we formally introduce them to the world of following directions or rules. Yet as children grow, they forget to bring homework home, don't follow the directions for the assignment, can't figure out why the recipe doesn't come out right, get ticketed for speeding, or are fired from jobs for constantly being late for work. Through activities, games, and sports, children soon learn that if they don't follow directions while moving and playing, then

- no one will want to play with them,
- they will not accomplish tasks to the best of their abilities,
- the group, class, or team may lose, and
- most important, their self-esteem will plummet.

Once children learn to follow directions at play, they can easily translate these skills to the classroom.

 • **Children need to think logically.** Young children live in the present; they do not have a mature sense of past or future. As a result, they need to learn how to analyze situations for deeper meaning. When teachers ask, "What do you think happened next?" students start to realize the importance of logical thinking. If children learn to accomplish physical tasks in a planned, rhythmic, and sequential manner, this skill will translate to their everyday thought processes. For example, just listen to kids who want to stay up past bedtime or skip eating the broccoli. If they have mastered logical thinking skills, they will come up with all sorts of negotiating strategies to achieve their goal.

 • **Children need to be able to transfer work to paper from an overhead or chalkboard.** All through life we are bombarded with data that we must transfer from one place to another. To do this, we must be aware of our physical relationship to other objects. To help children properly orient themselves to the objects that surround them, PFS stimulates spatial awareness through activities and games that place children in relationships with other children and objects.

 • **Children need to understand order.** Children cannot learn the alphabet or learn how to count without first understanding order, which is related to sequencing. Through simple sequencing games, activities, songs, and rhymes, children can learn to process things in an orderly manner.

 • **Children need to understand where to begin.** In a nationally respected reading clinic at Western Michigan University, the first thing children are taught when they begin to read is where to start on the page. Adults often take for granted that kids will begin reading or working math problems in the correct spot, but many children have no idea where to begin. For those with learning disabilities, this is even more difficult. Project First Step helps children gain internal awareness of top, bottom, right, left, front, and back.

• **Children need to feel that they can succeed.** Children who do not think they can succeed will expend little effort attempting to do so. Positive reinforcement is a PFS mainstay. All children must be doing *something* right; our task is to find that one thing and make the child aware of it. It might be as simple as "You really concentrated hard that time," or "You're really improving, you did it twice in a row." Success breeds success, and failure breeds failure.

• **Children need to be aware of their space and of the space of others.** Most people don't like it when someone else invades "their space," that little circle of comfort we all place around ourselves and our possessions. We hate to be pushed, bumped into, or have our things disturbed. Many children are not aware that they are walking into other children, knocking papers off desks, or crashing through doors. Activities such as "Keep Away" and negotiating obstacle courses help children to understand their relationship to surroundings.

• **Children need to feel comfortable.** Have you ever seen a baby who doesn't want to be held, a child who can't sit still, or a person who wears long sleeves when it's hot outside? Since tactile sensations are rooted deep inside the nervous system, such people are literally uncomfortable within their own skin. If students feel this way, there is a good chance they will not be able to learn very well, and may even develop discipline problems if teachers can't identify the reason for their discomfort. Because tactile experiences are acquired skills, they ordinarily begin with very light sensations, such as stroking and rocking a baby, and graduate to harder or rougher sensations, such as rolling on the ground or touching burlap. A child learns from big to little, head to feet, and inside of the body to outside the body (Roach & Kephart, 1966).

CONCLUSION

It was "Zoo Day" for the kindergartners. The animals from Binder Park Zoo were coming for a visit. The morning and afternoon classes were combined in the regular kindergarten room. With sixty excited youngsters, some parents, the teacher and aide, the principal, the animals and their trainers, the decibels in the room went off the chart. The principal tried all of the standard attention-getting techniques to no avail. The petite instructor tugged on her sleeve.

"Watch this," she said, before turning to her fellow students. "Put your hands on your head. Put your hands on your shoulders. Put your hands on your hips. Put your hands on your toes. Now be quiet and pay attention to the nice people from the zoo."

Suddenly, sixty little children, along with everyone else in the room, came under her control.

Through activities such as this one, Project First Step helps teach children to listen, balance, identify body parts, sequence, and many other skills. The students are unaware that they're doing anything academic because they are learning through play, which is just as well; after all, "learn it through play and it's there to stay" (Inskeep, 1926).

REFERENCES

Cratty, B. J. (1970). *Perceptual and motor development in infants and children.* Los Angeles: Macmillan.

Hedges, W. D., & Hardin, V. B. (1972). Effects of a perceptual-motor program on the achievement of first graders. *Educational Leadership, 30*(3), 249–253.

Inskeep, A. D. (1926). *Teaching dull and retarded children.* New York: The Macmillan Company.

Jensen, E. (1998). *Teaching with the brain in mind.* Alexandria, VA: Association for Supervision and Curriculum Development.

Kotulak, R. (1997). *Inside the brain.* Kansas City, MO: Andrews McMeel Publishing.

Levin, D. E. (1998). *Remote control childhood: Combating the hazards of media culture.* Washington, DC: National Association for the Education of Young Children.

Roach, E. G., & Kephart, N.C. (1966). *The Purdue perceptual motor survey.* Columbus, OH: Charles E. Merrill Publishing Company.

Schroeder, B. A. (1992). *Human growth and development.* St. Paul, MN: West Publishing.

Schurr, E. L. (1975). *Movement experiences for children.* Englewood Cliffs, NJ: Prentice-Hall.

Sprenger, M. (1999). *Learning and memory: The brain in action.* Alexandria, VA: Association for Supervision and Curriculum Development.

Steele, W. L. (1976). *Project Adapt: 2nd year final report, ESEA, Title III.* Washington, DC: U.S. Department of Education.

Winn, M. (1985). *The plug-in drug: Television, children, and the family.* New York: Penguin Books.

THE CLASSROOM
OF YOUR DREAMS

Jim Fay

Have you ever seen a classroom that runs so smoothly that the teacher spends most of the day teaching—not disciplining—and students feel secure knowing they'll be treated with respect by everyone? And have you seen a very different classroom in which the teacher could make the best kid in town misbehave? I saw both these classrooms on the same day.

Recently I was visiting a school and lingered by two classrooms on my way toward the office. The teacher in the first room appeared to have had her finger in the light socket too long: She looked frazzled. Her voice had an edge to it, and the volume increased by the second. I heard her saying, "Young man, your name is on the board, and in one minute you're getting your third check mark, and you know what that means! I mean it this time!" The student responded with the obligatory eye rolling and "So?"

The more I watched, the more I could see that she was spending far more time putting out little brush fires and dealing with problems than teaching. The kids were testing her constantly. I'm not sure I heard her complete a sentence without inserting "Shhh" at least once. It was painful to watch, and I wondered if I wanted to spend more time in this school.

But as luck would have it, I spied the classroom across the hall. There I saw kids with smiles on their faces, involved with their teacher in positive ways, helping each other in groups, and generally acting as though they liked being in school.

The teacher in this room had a smile on her face. Her voice was soft and pleasant. She was actually spending her time instructing the kids instead of dealing with problems. I thought it would be interesting to spend more time in this room. I sneaked in and sat in the back for the rest of the lesson.

Soon it was time for recess, so I tagged along. I walked up to the teacher while she supervised recess and asked, "How do you have so much fun and get the kids to behave the way they do? I mean, this is supposed to be a tough school."

"If you have time for a story, I'd love to tell you how it all came about," she answered. Then she described a transformation that occurred for her and changed her professional life.

THE EVOLUTION OF A "LOVE AND LOGIC" CLASSROOM

"One of the teachers at a local school attended the Rocky Mountain Conference last summer. I couldn't believe how excited she was about what she learned. She was so thrilled with how the approach from the book *Teaching with Love and Logic* (Fay & Funk, 1998) worked for her that she held a workshop for the rest of us so we could learn about it and be part of her study group. I was especially interested since my classroom used to operate just like the one across the hall, and I was considering changing professions. I had run out of threats, warnings, lectures, and rewards, and I needed to make some changes."

I NOTIFIED MY PRINCIPAL

"I took the advice I got at this workshop about going to my principal first. I explained that I wanted to run some experiments with the techniques I had just learned. I pointed out some of the experiments in the book and told him that I wanted to take more responsibility for my own discipline. He was excited when he found that it would mean less work for him. Needless to say, we could both see the value in the kids thinking of me, not the principal, as their authority figure."

I EXPERIMENTED WITH ONE TECHNIQUE AT A TIME

"The best advice I got was to start slowly by experimenting with, and mastering, only one technique at a time. My kids were constantly arguing with me, so I was eager to experiment with a Love and Logic technique designed to put an end to this. I put up a sign that read, 'ARGUING TIME IS 12:15 and 3:15 DAILY.' I made the sign look real friendly with little happy faces. When kids would try to argue, I'd just point at the sign with a smile and a questioning look. I felt a little control moving back to me in the classroom. Arguing wasn't working! I began to avoid using fighting words like 'You must,' 'Right now,' and 'What's the matter with you?'

"It was a struggle at first, but I began using enforceable statements like, 'I'll be calling on kids who raise their hands,' and 'I'll be lining people up as soon as it is quiet,' and 'All those who remember permission slips may come on the field trip.'

"Now I was hooked; I was ready to experiment with anticipatory consequences. I used to fear that I wouldn't know what to do, but now I was lying in ambush for a discipline problem to erupt in my classroom. With Love and Logic, I actually started looking forward to kids misbehaving.

"Suddenly my fondest hopes were realized: Before my eyes I saw Jason passing notes. I descended upon him with a smile instead of my usual frown and, with all the kindness I could muster, I took the note and said, 'This is sad. I'm going to need to do something about this, but I don't have time now since I'm busy teaching.' I told him that I'd get back to him on this subject later and that he should try not to worry about it during class time. He was shocked and started demanding to know what I was going to do. But I just pointed to my sign about arguing time.

"This was the first time in my career that I didn't stop my instruction to deal with a problem. It was the first time I didn't feel at a loss about how to handle the situation. I knew that I could visit with my colleagues during planning time and that I could let Jason stew about his dilemma until I was ready to deal with him on my own terms.

"During my planning time, I got my friends to help design a suitable consequence. Then I did something I had never done before. I went to my principal and made sure that I had the necessary support to do what I needed to do. My teacher friends, the principal, and I were now a team.

"By the time I finally told Jason what I was going to do about his note passing, he had already thought of several ways he could solve the problem as well. And the wonderful thing about this approach is that when I met with Jason to tell him his consequence, I was totally calm and quite empathetic. This is something I couldn't do before. Why? Because I had tried to deal with a discipline problem during the heat of emotion without knowing whether or not I had the support of the rest of the staff.

"I found it exhilarating to be in control of my own emotions while dealing with a problem that used to frustrate me. I believe my new behavior that day sent a powerful message to Jason as well as to the rest of the class. It was a message that I cared for the kids, but I could provide structure and boundaries. That was the day my classroom management took on a new life."

I LEARNED TO LOCK IN EMPATHY
BEFORE DESCRIBING A CONSEQUENCE

"This incident with Jason taught me another important lesson—that when adults do a good job of expressing their compassion and empathy before decreeing a consequence, the child's main focus is upon his or her bad decision or behavior as opposed to the anger of the adult. I knew it was important to blend consequences with empathy, but I sometimes found it difficult to even think of an empathetic statement when I was upset with a student.

"Fortunately, some of the other teachers were more practiced at using Love and Logic than I was, and they taught me to practice using the same empathetic response every time. I settled on 'That's sad.' My empathetic response to statements like these kept me from ranting, raving and lecturing.

I lost my homework. 'That's sad. What are you going to do?'

Billy's bothering me again. 'That's sad. Do you think you can solve the problem on your own?'

Jason was passing notes again. 'That's so sad. We'll deal with this later. Try not to worry about it.'

"By the end of the following day, my students were in shock. 'Where was that teacher who used to get so angry, putting on those elaborate and spectacular shows filled with lectures and idle threats? This new teacher is concerned for us and tries to help us stay out of trouble.'

"This is one of the greatest techniques I have ever learned. In less than a month the climate in my room became calm. Calm replaced chaos. The quality of my relationships with the children was unbelievably better."

I LEARNED THE POWER OF DISCIPLINARY INTERVENTIONS

"I started listening to audio tapes in the car as I traveled to work. They helped me review my plans for dealing with student behavior. I began to feel more confident. It was fun to pick just one of these ideas to experiment with each day. I'll never forget the day that I walked up to Audrey and whispered in her ear, 'Audrey, could you save that behavior for Mr. Morgan's class? Thank you.' Audrey grinned from ear to ear and got back to work. It was so easy that I almost started laughing out loud. I silently patted myself on the back. Audrey wasn't in trouble, and I didn't have to make a big deal out of it. I was so proud of my new techniques. I shared this with Mr. Morgan. He just chuckled and said, 'Okay, if she does it in my room, I'll pass it back to you.' "

I BEGAN TO QUESTION MY OLD DISCIPLINE PLAN

"At one time, I believed that I needed a rule for every conceivable student misbehavior. I began to question this, realizing that I had many rules that I could not enforce. I became painfully aware of this fact the afternoon that I descended upon Philip and Jerome, who were beginning to fight. I said, 'You guys keep your hands to yourselves. You know the rules. I don't want to see you touching each other again. I mean it!'

"I turned my back to walk away and heard the dreaded, 'Oooooooh,' from the class. One kid yelled, 'Now they're hugging each other!' I turned to see both kids hugging and grinning. At that moment it hit me that kids know that there are certain things others have no control over. I realized that I made a big dent in my credibility each time I made a rule over which I had no control.

"That was the day I decided to take a close look at my classroom rules to discover which ones I could control and which were simply wishes. I found that I had control only over my own actions and muscles. The kids have control over their actions and muscles. Telling kids to keep their hands to themselves was not something I could control. But I could control what I did about their touching each other.

"I decided to change the way I talked to kids. I learned to set firm limits using more positive words by stating what 'I' may do. That's why you'll hear me saying to the class, 'I'll be taking kids who have their coats with me to recess.' I have control over who I take. I used to say, 'Get your coats on before you go to recess.' That's why I had so much trouble before. The kids love to test someone who tries to order them around."

I CREATED A NEW DISCIPLINE POLICY FOR MY ROOM

"Now that I was armed with some new skills, I was ready to do away with check marks on the board and my point system. I wanted a new discipline plan that put the responsibility on the students instead of on my shoulders. Once more I approached the principal with my plan, assuring him that I could handle my discipline without making a problem for administrators.

"The next morning I opened class with a discussion of classroom rules and consequences.

" 'Kids, I think we no longer need this long list of classroom rules and this long list of consequences. I think a couple of rules are enough. Let me write the new rules on the board.' I wrote

- Rule Number One: I'll treat you with respect so you'll know how to treat me.
- Rule Number Two: You can do whatever you want as long as it doesn't make a problem for others.
- Rule Number Three: If you make a problem for others, you will be expected to solve that problem without making a problem for anyone else, including your parents.

"Now let me write the new consequence list on the board," I continued. *'If you make a problem and don't solve that problem, I will do something.'*

"What are you going to do?" the kids asked. I said, 'How should I know. I have to wait and see what you do and then I will figure it out. You need to know that I treat all situations differently, and all people differently because we are all different. I will try to be fair. If I ever do something that isn't fair, I want you to come to me in private and say these words. Let me write them on the board. *'I'm not sure that's fair.'*

"I had the entire class practice saying that sentence until they had it down pat. Then I made a little sign to put up in my room (see Figure 16.1).

"Now that I was committed to a new approach to classroom discipline, I needed to explain it to the parents. I sent a letter home with the kids" (see Figure 16.2).

FIGURE 16.1

MY GUARANTEE OF FAIRNESS

If you think that you have been treated unfairly,
Come to me and say, 'I'm not sure that's fair.'
Present your ideas in a nice way,
And if you present a good case,
I will change the consequence so it fits better.

Signed,
Mrs. Flint

FIGURE 16.2

LETTER TO PARENTS

Dear Parents,

I have been refining my approach to discipline. The purpose of this letter is to share my beliefs about working with children, and it can be considered my personal "code of ethics" relating to how I conduct myself when dealing with disciplinary problems.

Rules in my classroom are few. I believe that as all children are different and all actions and reactions are personal in nature, effective discipline involves a few overriding tenets rather than a long list of specific rules. Situations are dealt with as they arise, with the focus on enabling the child to grow and learn from his or her actions.

* * * * *

Guidelines for Student Behavior

1. You may engage in any behavior that does not create a problem for you or anyone else in the world.
2. If you find yourself with a problem, you may solve it by any means that do not cause a problem for anyone else in the world.
3. You may engage in any behavior that does not jeopardize the safety or learning of yourself or others. Unkind words and actions will not be tolerated.

* * * * *

In ensuring that the above guidelines are adhered to, I will operate with the following principles as my guide:

1. I will react without anger or haste to problem situations.
2. I will provide consequences that are not punitive but that allow the child to experience the results of a poor choice, enabling him or her to make better choices in the future.
3. I will proceed in all situations with the best interest of the whole child foremost in my mind. Academic, social, and emotional well-being will be fostered.
4. I will guide students toward personal responsibility and the decision-making skills they will need to function in the real world.
5. I will arrange consequences for problem situations in such a way that the child will not be humiliated or demeaned.

continued

FIGURE 16.2
CONTINUED

6. Equal is not always fair. Consequences will be designed to fit the problems of individual students, and they may be different even when problems appear to be the same.
7. I will make every effort to ensure that, in each situation, the students involved understand why they are involved in consequences.
8. If at any time I act or react in a way that a child truly feels is unjust, that student need only say to me, "I'm not sure that's fair." I will arrange a private conference during which the student can express to me why he or she feels my actions were not fair. This may or may not change my course of action. I am always open to calm, rational discussion of any matter.

Note: Credit must be given to Amy Krochmal, a second-year teacher who created the original of this letter in 1996. She has given permission for others to copy and use this letter. It has been an inspiration to many teachers.

It was time for recess to end. Mrs. Flint gave a call and then started toward the school. The students gave up their play and fell in behind her, ready to follow this teacher who treated them with love and respect, yet who held high expectations and set clear limits for her students.

As they returned to class, I thought how lucky they all were to have each other. I thought how many parents would want such a teacher for their children. As she went through the door, Mrs. Flint waved and smiled, then returned to the job she once again loved.

REFERENCES

Fay, J., & Funk, D. (1998). *Teaching with love and logic.* Golden, CO: Love and Logic Press.

THREE STORIES FROM HUNTINGTON WOODS SCHOOL: IMPLEMENTING THE CONDITIONS TO ACHIEVE QUALITY LEARNING

Kaye Mentley and Sally Ludwig

Huntington Woods Elementary School, in the Wyoming Public Schools system in Michigan, has been designed to be a place where all students can learn successfully without labeling or special programs (Ludwig & Mentley, 1997). And we are reaching this goal. At this writing, with full inclusion, 100 percent of 5th graders and 98 percent of 2nd graders are reading at or above grade level. The faculty chose William Glasser's principles of the Quality School as our design model (Glasser, 1992, 1993, 1998, 2000).

To achieve quality learning, some conditions must be met—conditions that are simple, but profound. The first condition is an environment of warm, supportive relationships, free from fear and from coercion of children or adults. In this climate, everyone in the school can meet the basic human needs of safety and survival, belonging, power, recognition, freedom, and fun. To help build strong relationships among teachers, students, and parents, students are grouped full time in multi-age learning families, each with two teachers and a teacher assistant, that stay together for three

Note: The William Glasser Institute can be contacted at 22024 Lassen Street, Suite 118, Chatsworth, CA 91311; phone 800-898-0688; fax 818-700-0555; http://www.wglasserinst.com.

years. Classrooms are open to parents at all times. Parents are our strongest supporters, assisting in classrooms and participating in all aspects of the school. There is extensive use of class meetings, cooperative learning, and student-to-student tutoring to enhance learning and to strengthen friendships and interpersonal acceptance.

The school calendar and schedule have been designed to be advantageous for learning and professional development. Students attend school during 11 months of each year, with a five-week break in July and August. Six weeks of optional, thematic intersession classes are offered within that extended calendar, providing more than 200 days of instruction for students who attend all intersessions. The traditional weekly schedule has been altered by lengthening the students' days Monday through Thursday and shortening the day on Friday, when students are dismissed at noon. This provides the time necessary for our teacher teams to learn, grow, and plan together. Each learning family flexibly schedules its own recess and lunch periods.

The second condition for quality is useful, meaningful learning that students recognize will make their lives better. For the most developmentally appropriate instruction, we rely on teacher-designed lessons and units, rather than textbooks, and emphasize hands-on learning activities. Content focuses on the skills of speaking, reading and writing, math calculation, and problem solving. Students are frequently asked what they would like to learn. It is then the teachers' jobs to determine how to teach state and district curriculum objectives within the topics the children want to study. The teacher takes the role of lead-manager who facilitates learning, while the role of the child is that of active, self-directed learner.

For reading, we use Owen's Literacy Learning strategies (Smith, 1997). This program, developed in New Zealand for classroom use, parallels the concept of Reading Recovery (Clay, 1985). Technology is used for self-directed learning through the Integrated Learning System (ILS) on our networked computers. Using the ILS software, students are assessed on basic skills and then given appropriate lessons based on the assessment result.

The third condition for quality, self-evaluation for continual improvement, is used by both students and staff. The process of self-evaluation is one of the most important skills we can offer to our students. Students are taught from the earliest grades to assess their performance in both school work and behavior and decide how they can improve it. Teachers involve students in developing goals and setting criteria for high-quality achievement. If children wish to improve their work at any time, any grade can be raised. As the school year progresses, students create portfolios containing examples of their schoolwork that demonstrate what they are learning and how they are using their knowledge. With teacher help, each student plans and rehearses a conference with his or her parents or guardians, then hosts the conference and presents the portfolio work in a way appropriate to his or her development. Students then tell their parents about how the projects were done and how they have been improved. Each student explains what was learned and how it can be applied, and describes plans for further learning. Parents and teachers offer their feedback and suggestions, discussing a plan for helping the student progress and deciding how they will help at home and at school.

All problems are solved by talking them through. No punishments or rewards are used. Rather, students learn to evaluate what they want and to plan the most effective, responsible way to get it. This method, integrated with strong, need-satisfying relationships within a supportive system, is successful in eliminating major discipline problems.

Adults at Huntington also use self-evaluation extensively rather than being evaluated by supervisors. As part of our self-evaluation as educators, we learn from our students. The three stories we have chosen to share are examples of children who have helped us learn and relearn ways to improve our teaching.

AMY'S STORY

When Amy entered kindergarten at our school, she was a cute, curly-headed little girl. Her parents were recent immigrants who spoke little English. It was difficult to tell how much or how little English Amy spoke because she hardly talked to her teachers or to the other children. Her teachers were confident, though, that she would soon become comfortable in her classroom and interested in the things going on there.

But Amy did not get involved in classroom learning activities. She only liked to play, and her play was very aggressive. If another child had a toy she wanted, she snatched it away. If the child objected, she hit, kicked, or beat up that child. When the teacher intervened, Amy ran away from her, sometimes running out of the classroom and, more than once, out of the school.

Amy also caught head lice and was sent home for treatment three times. Her parents got so frustrated that they shaved Amy's head, so she had to come to school bald.

School was becoming more and more a series of negative experiences for Amy. We expected her to adjust and follow the school rules, but because she did not choose the behaviors we wanted, our interactions with her grew more and more negative. We continued to be nice to her, greeting her every morning and so on, as we do with all the children, but it wasn't long until we were feeling less than patient. Then we forgot to think at all about the quality of the relationship. Our only focus was on how could we get Amy to do what we wanted her to do.

We tried different methods—isolating her from other kids, giving her time-outs, removing her from the classroom to the principal's office, even sending her home a couple of times when she ran away from her teachers—all of which resulted in absolutely no improvement. We had frequent meetings of her teachers, the principal, the school psychologist, and everybody we could think of to try to figure out how to change Amy's behavior. People suggested various things; we tried them, but none worked. We even recruited Amy's older cousin, also a student at the school, to talk to her and ask her to behave; Amy ran away from him, too. Talking with her parents did not help. The language barrier made communication difficult, but a bigger obstacle was the school's relationship with the family. Their experience with us had been predominately negative as we had called to tell them that Amy had contracted lice, had hit a child, or had again run out of the school. All this time, no academic learning was going on. She was not learning letters, numbers, social skills, or any of the other things her classmates were learning.

Finally, in one of our many meetings, one of her teachers said, "We have to stop. Everything we are doing and talking about doing is focusing on the negative in Amy. We have to start loving her and showing her that we love her and figure out what will help her be happy in school. Until we do that, her behavior will stay the same, and she won't start to learn anything." We knew that the teacher was right. So, at the next staff meeting, all of us talked about ways to help the school develop a better relationship with Amy. We asked the teachers, teaching assistants, secretary, custodian, and food service staff to greet her when they saw her in the hall and to never criticize her, but rather make positive comments to her. We even went so far as to ask that if they saw Amy running down the hall away from her classroom, they should say only, "Good morning, Amy." Everyone agreed to do this.

For a period of about one week, everyone was very friendly toward Amy, and she started to respond. When a teacher saw her running down the hall and greeted her warmly, Amy would say, "Good morning!" as she ran past. As we continued to extend friendship to her, she became more open with us and more talkative. Then at the next staff meeting, we decided on our next goal—to find some things Amy liked that we might be able to incorporate into her school morning. One day her teacher asked her, "Amy, if you could do anything you wanted to here at school, what would you do?" Amy said, "I would clean." Surprised, the teacher asked why she wanted to clean and what she would clean. Amy said that she liked to clean. Not only was this one of her big responsibilities at home, but she also thought the school was too messy!

So the teacher and Amy put together a schedule of cleaning duties for her. We knew that letting Amy spend time doing something she enjoyed and was good at would help her meet her need for power (achievement and recognition). We also knew from her tendency to run out of the class so often that she had a high need for freedom. Our goal for her cleaning was to help Amy meet her needs for power and freedom. She did most of her new job in the classroom, dusting bookshelves and countertops, washing out the sink, polishing the faucets, washing the tabletops, and straightening books on the shelves.

Because we knew Amy had such a high need for freedom, we took a big risk and incorporated into her cleaning schedule the task of washing dishes in the teachers' lounge, which meant that she would leave the classroom by herself. We thought it important that we not accompany her, so Amy would know we trusted her to do her job. It would better meet her freedom need if no adults were supervising her. All by herself, she went down the hallway, around the corner to the next hallway, and into the teachers' lounge. One of the teachers brought a stepstool from home so that Amy could reach the sink. In the lounge, she pushed the stool over to the sink, gathered all the coffee mugs and silverware, ran the water, and put in a more-than-generous squirt of dishwashing liquid (she loved bubbles). She washed and rinsed every piece and set everything out on a towel to dry. Then she rinsed the sink, wiped off the table, put her stool away, and returned to the classroom. Later in the morning, she told her teacher when she thought the dishes were dry and ready to be put away, and she went by herself to finish her work.

We gave Amy total control over when and how she would do this project, and on some mornings she made five or six trips to the lounge. But she did become happier in school and much friendlier to the other students. Soon she began to make some friends in the classroom and didn't want to leave as often. After two weeks, she was leaving class to go to the lounge perhaps two or three times per morning. We noticed that often while she was cleaning, Amy worked her way closer and closer to where the lesson was taking place. And she was listening—we found that she was learning much more than we realized at first. Sometimes when the teachers asked a question, Amy answered it, or even entered the discussion, from where she stood dusting the bookshelves or cleaning the countertop. Then came times, more and more often, when she chose to join the group.

All this occurred in December and January. By the end of the school year, Amy had achieved all of her grade-level academic standards, was conversing well, and had several friends in the class. She liked her teachers very much and, most important, she liked school. In addition to cleaning, she volunteered for several more jobs in the classroom. By spring, when adult visitors came to the room, Amy would walk up and greet them (in very good English), welcome them to the class, and volunteer to answer any questions they had.

SOME LESSONS WE LEARNED FROM AMY

• Even though we know how to form good relationships and how to help children to like school, when we were faced with a difficult student and things were going badly, we reverted to our old, more coercive ways of behaving. As Amy's teacher finally realized, we needed to stop all that and start loving her. We knew that what we had been doing was not working, and we all resolved to do whatever we could to help Amy. Adopting this unanimously as a whole-staff attitude helped us. Everyone committed to greeting Amy and speaking positively to her, and no one objected to her presence in the lounge. At that point, she began to change her behavior. Also, the teachers really appreciated the clean coffee mugs and silverware!

• Although we were having difficulty with Amy's behavior, if we had really started punishing her, we probably could have made things so bad for Amy that she would have sat quietly in the group. Coercion (forcing or bribing somebody to do what want we want them to) often does get compliance. But it is only that—compliance, for the sake of avoiding punishment or getting rewards, not cooperation. By strengthening our relationships with Amy and focusing on her needs, we instead saw her come to love school and love learning.

ANDREW'S STORY

Andrew comes from a nice, advantaged, upper-middle-class, two-parent family. Everything seemed fine for him in kindergarten, where he was a pleasant little boy who liked coming to school. Once he was in 1st grade, though, his parents and teachers began to express concern because Andy wasn't learning to read. At first we thought, "Well, he's young, and a boy, and might start more slowly. We just need to be patient and continue the classroom instruction." After several months, though, there still wasn't much progress, so we began to intensify our efforts. We did the things that usually help our later readers get off to a good start—having the teaching assistants work with him for extra instruction during the day, having him listen to books on tape, giving his parents activities to do with him at home, providing extra phonics lessons, giving him choices of varied reading materials, scheduling more reading lessons on the computer, and doubling the amount of reading instructional time he got during the day by having him attend two reading groups. We continued that until the end of the school year.

As we proceeded with more intensive instructional efforts, our formerly happy Andy began liking school less. He started acting out during class and sometimes did not want to participate. His parents also reported that some days he did not want to come to school. This concerned us a great deal. He was not improving in reading as most of our students do with the intensive work, and he was losing his joyful approach. Andy's family valued education greatly, so his parents were also experiencing some stress over his decline in attitude.

When it was time for him to start 2nd grade, we knew we had to do something different to get back the happy student we had had and to help Andrew learn to read. We had just begun work with a developmental optometrist, and over the summer had trained two of our paraprofessionals in vision therapy. That fall, when the optometrist did a vision screening, he discovered that Andy's eyes were not working well together. With this finding, we began to better understand both his difficulty with reading and his change in attitude. We had been continually asking him to do something that, in spite of his best efforts, he could not do.

So, we stopped teaching reading to Andy (which was a scary step to take) and instead began providing daily vision therapy. By February, his eye coordination and movement had improved so much that he was ready to begin reading instruction. By the end of the school year, Andy was reading above grade level and loving it. He was again happy in school and ready to go on to the upper elementary level. Andy's parents were thrilled, not only about his progress, but also about the way our staff continued to search for things that would work without blaming their son or accepting his failure. They had so much confidence in us and in the quality of their children's learning with us, that even after the family moved to a community 15 miles away, they continued (and, a year later, still continue) to drive Andy and their other three children to Huntington Woods every day.

SOME LESSONS WE LEARNED FROM ANDREW

• We cannot and should not ask children to do something they are not developmentally ready to do. In their efforts to please us, children will develop more serious learning problems.

• When we realize that a student is not ready for a particular task or subject, such as reading, it is not our job just to wait until he is ready. There are specific things we can do to *help* children develop and get ready to learn. Children at all developmental levels can learn in a general education setting, and there are things that all students need in order to be ready to read. Young children's reading performance will be strengthened if early elementary teachers incorporate activities to help students develop balance; gross-motor, fine-motor, and oculomotor skills; spatial relationships; and visual memory (see Fig. 17.1).

• Problems in these areas are fixable and best addressed early in kindergarten or 1st grade to ensure that school is a positive experience for children. This approach is much more successful than later heroic efforts to change children who have already failed to learn for several years, who see themselves as unable to learn, and who are likely unwilling to try any more.

TOMMY'S STORY

As a 2nd-grader, Tommy was diagnosed with a learning disability in reading. He was given many kinds of instruction and encouraged to take part in our before-school reading clinic. We met with his mother to share ways she could help him at home. In spite of all our efforts, Tommy did not

FIGURE 17.1
PUSHPIN EXERCISE

For each student, take a page out of a coloring book and attach it to a sheet of foam board. Using a pushpin, the student must then punch holes around the outline of the picture. This activity helps young children develop focusing, converging and tracking skills, all of which are necessary to reading.

For more information on vision therapy, contact Livingston Developmental Academy, 9758 E. Highland Rd., Howell, MI 48843; phone: 810-632-2200.

make progress in reading. As he grew older, he began to goof off more and more in school, and his attendance became sporadic.

On a couple of occasions, we spoke with Tommy's mother and reminded her that her son qualified as learning disabled and that if she wanted to, she had a right to put him into a special education program. We shared with her our evidence that Tommy was not making progress in reading. On each occasion, his mom said she wanted to keep him at Huntington Woods and see what happened. (She may have made that choice, not because she believed that Huntington is a terrific school and that the teachers would figure things out, but rather because it is a year-round school. She is a single mom, and needed a no-cost place for Tommy to spend his days in the summer.) At each of these meetings, we encouraged her to improve Tommy's attendance at school, his participation in the optional reading clinic, and her work with him at home. At each occasion she agreed, but she did not follow through.

In the fall of Tommy's 5th-grade year, his reading tests showed him to be reading at a beginning 2nd-grade level. The principal and I met with Tommy and asked about his plans for middle school. In our district, students can choose between two schools when they start 6th grade, and Tommy indicated that he preferred one of them. I said, "That sounds like a good choice for you. But Tommy, I want you to understand that you will not be promoted to middle school until you are reading well. It's okay with us if you stay here until you're a lot older, because we love you a lot, and we would like to have you here longer. We will help you, and when your reading is strong, then you can go to middle school." I shared the results of Tommy's most recent reading test with him so that he had a good idea of how he was performing. I reviewed some of the things the school would do to help him read—extra tutoring, the before-school reading clinic, providing lots of reading materials at his current level, frequent testing to monitor his progress, time available daily for silent reading, and computer-assisted instruction. Then I asked what he was willing to do in order to improve his reading. Tommy didn't say much at the time.

He must have given the matter some thought, though, because soon after our talk he began attending the reading clinic regularly and putting forth more effort during in-class instruction. As he did, we continually complimented Tommy on his efforts. We let him take assessments any time he wished so that he could see when he had moved up in our program of leveled readers. By April of that year, Tommy was reading solidly at grade level and was extremely proud of himself. He often talked with other students about his reading and shared with his friends the importance of attending the reading clinic daily and working hard.

SOME LESSONS WE LEARNED FROM TOMMY

- Expectations are vital. It is important not only to hold high expectations for students, but also to communicate those expectations clearly to them. We continue to follow the advice of Dr. Glasser, who has often said, "Never give up" on a child.
- In an atmosphere of unconditional love for students, sometimes direct confrontation can be very effective. With the first condition for quality in place, an environment of friendly relationships without fear or coercion, I could confront Tommy as an invitation to self-evaluate rather than as a threat. He knew already that I cared about him, had his welfare at heart, and would support him in the choices he made.
- Until Tommy saw reading and the reading clinic as useful to him (the second condition for quality), he had no interest in trying hard or attending regularly. Once he perceived better reading skills as something he wanted, he became a willing, hard-working learner. He took advantage of all the opportunities offered for instruction and practice and improved rapidly.
- Tommy's self-evaluation (the third condition for quality) was a turning point for him. Once he decided in his own mind that he really wanted to be a better reader, and he realized that what he was doing was not helping him get what he wanted, he became willing to make the necessary effort. He then evaluated his performance each day, assessing whether it was moving him closer to his goal and whether he was putting forth his best effort. We provided support, tools, and feedback to help him self-evaluate accurately.

By carefully and consistently implementing these conditions for quality, we create an environment in which the vast majority of our students learn well and love school. In addition, we have earned a great deal of parental support and trust. By examining our choices with the few students who are still having difficulty with learning and behavior, we continue to find ways to improve our school.

REFERENCES

Clay, M. M. (1985). *The early detection of reading difficulties* (3rd ed.). Portsmouth, NH: Heinemann.

Glasser, W. (1992). *The quality school: Managing students without coercion.* New York: HarperCollins.

Glasser, W. (1993). *The quality school teacher: A companion volume to The Quality School.* New York: HarperCollins.

Glasser, W. (1998). *Choice theory: A new psychology of personal freedom.* New York: HarperCollins.

Glasser, W. (2000). *Every student can succeed.* Chatsworth, CA: The William Glasser Institute.

Ludwig, S., & Mentley, K. (1997). *Quality is the key: Stories from Huntington Woods School.* Wyoming, MI: KWM Educational Services, 12055 S. Woodwinds Circle #16, Traverse City, MI 49684.

Smith, J. W. A. (1997). *How children learn to read.* Katonah, NY: Richard C. Owen Publishers, Inc.

"JIMMY":
THE POWER OF PARENT-
TEACHER COOPERATION

Bob Sornson

After 22 years of teaching and the experience of raising four sons of her own, Mrs. Peterson still loved every day in the classroom. She had taught every grade from K through 5, but 2nd grade was her love. The sparkling eyes, developing skills, and emerging awareness of the 7- and 8-year-olds filled her with fascination and awe. Serving these children gave her the deepest sense of satisfaction, and this year one boy needed special attention.

Mrs. Peterson watched the group of boys intently as they raced around the playground. Jimmy's blue jacket was open and it flapped as he ran. Two boys ran after him, yelling, with angry looks. Mrs. Peterson sighed, then started walking out to meet them.

Jimmy was fast and all the kids knew it, but this time Josh and Jacob were persistent. Jimmy slowed down long enough to turn and yell.

"Suckers," he called. He hadn't noticed the agile stride of Mrs. Peterson as she walked along the outside wall of the school. He turned to resume running, and she was there.

"Hi, Jimmy." She took his hand.

Josh and Jacob continued to run toward them, and Mrs. Peterson continued to hold Jimmy's hand. These boys weren't exactly angels, either.

"He pushed me in the mud," said Josh in a voice filled with indignation. "We weren't even playing with him."

"I know," said Mrs. Peterson.

"I yelled at him, and he spit in my face," said Jacob. There were tears in his eyes.

"I know," said Mrs. Peterson. "I saw." She held Jimmy's hand. She looked at the other boys.

"Today, I'm going to handle this problem. Can you get over your anger and play outside today?"

They looked at her and nodded, then started to walk toward the play tower.

"I didn't," muttered Jimmy.

Didn't what? wondered Mrs. Peterson, but she held her tongue. Holding Jimmy's hand, she headed back to her classroom.

"I didn't do anything," grumbled Jimmy aloud as they walked.

She didn't comment or argue. Jimmy walked willingly with her.

In the month she had known Jimmy in class, she had become more concerned. It wasn't his restlessness. She'd known many fidgety boys. It wasn't the way he sometimes fell out of his chair, or the difficulty he had holding a pencil, or his poor reading skills. He used language pretty well, even if he sometimes misunderstood 2nd-grade humor. Somehow she knew he was smart enough.

It was the second day of school when she had started to worry, when he looked straight at her and said, "I don't have to do what you say." They crossed that bridge, and then it was a week later that he walked out of class without asking.

"What are you doing?" she asked him after three quick steps into the hall.

"I'm going to find a bathroom."

"We have our own bathroom," she responded.

"Matthew was just in there," Jimmy replied, glaring at her. "Now it stinks."

It was that look he sometimes had that bothered her. At other times, it was gone, and there were many times when he pushed close to her for warmth or security. Then his look was different.

Reaching the classroom, they hung up their coats and sat down at the back table.

"It was an accident," he told her.

"What was?" Mrs. Peterson asked.

"Pushing him down."

"How about the spitting?" she asked, but he was silent. He glared at the table.

"It's a problem for me when you hurt others," she explained, not for the first time. "Any ideas about how you can solve this problem?"

Already in the first month they'd had this conversation several times. She didn't expect an answer.

"I'm going to call your mom," she explained as she walked to the phone by her desk. After Mrs. Peterson explained the problem to Jimmy's mother on the phone, there was silence.

"I'm hoping you can come in," said Mrs. Peterson, breaking the silence.

"Do you mean right now?" said Jimmy's mother. "I can't come now. I can't just leave work."

"No, no," said Mrs. Peterson. "Things are fine now. Could you come in after school, or would evening be better?"

They decided on an evening meeting, and at 7:00 p.m. Mrs. Peterson had coffee and tea ready. A few minutes later, Mrs. Jackson arrived and, as she entered the 2nd-grade classroom, Mrs. Peterson thought how tired she looked. For a few minutes they talked about her work, and the fact that Jimmy was her only child.

"I'm worried about some of his behaviors at school," said Mrs. Peterson. "Could you tell me how the school year is going from your perspective at home?"

The younger woman looked worried. "Are you getting ready to start kicking him out every day? Please tell me the truth—is that going to happen again? Last year I almost lost my job."

Mrs. Peterson took a deep breath and looked with care at her. Tired, worried about Jimmy, concerned that others might think she's an inadequate mother, and strong, Mrs. Peterson noted. There was a strength of character and a commitment to one little boy that she saw in Mrs. Jackson's face.

"No," she responded. "I haven't considered that yet. And I sincerely hope I don't have to. I'm hoping we can work together this year and help Jimmy have a much better experience."

"He likes you so far. He really does," said Mrs. Jackson.

"Thank you. I'm very fond of him."

"My neighbor says I should fight for a Section 504 plan so I could make it much harder for the school to suspend him."

"Really? Do you think that might help?"

"Well, she's had two boys who had an awful time in school and she says a mother just has to fight for anything."

"That's so sad," said Mrs. Peterson. For a moment there was silence.

"Do you think I should?" asked Mrs. Jackson sincerely.

"Maybe some day. I can't rule that out for you. But I'm hoping we can find some other options right now."

"I heard you were really good with boys. I asked to have Jimmy put into your class. Did you know that?"

Mrs. Peterson nodded.

"I'll bet you wish I hadn't."

Mrs. Peterson pulled her chair closer to the young woman. She wanted no table between them.

"Did you think I wanted you here tonight to tell you what a bad kid Jimmy is?"

Mrs. Jackson nodded slightly, but did not speak. Mrs. Peterson went on. "Would you like to work with me?"

"What do you mean?"

"Shall we work together this year for as long as it takes to help Jimmy get his behavior and his attention working better? It'll be a lot of work."

"You'd teach me what to do at home?"

Mrs. Peterson smiled. "Everything I can. And if we need help, we'll find it. We can meet here every Monday night, just like this, and we'll develop a plan for home and school."

"You'd do that for me?"

"And for Jimmy," the teacher responded.

A little of the tiredness faded from the young woman's face as they talked that night. The night janitor walked by the room a couple of times and smiled. He'd heard about Jimmy, and knew of the other parents Mrs. Peterson had helped in the past.

The first thing they planned to work on at home was getting Jimmy to go to recovery time ("time out") without a fight. Mrs. Peterson gave Jimmy's mother an audio tape to study.

"Don't try to change much this week," cautioned Mrs. Peterson. "Let's go slowly and get it right."

* * * * *

The following Monday, the two women met again. They shared coffee and smiles and concerns.

"Twice I had to take him to his room for recovery time," recalled Mrs. Jackson. "Then yesterday when I told him we needed a little recovery time, he went all by himself."

"For how long?"

"He was quiet and thinking, so I went to the door after four minutes and told him to feel free to come out whenever he was feeling sweet."

"Did he come out right away?"

"No," Julie Jackson laughed. "I think he wanted to hold on to a little control over when he came out. But a few minutes later he came out and snuggled next to me on the couch."

"I'll bet that felt good," said Mrs. Peterson.

"Yes. He seemed calm." Mrs. Jackson paused. "I really haven't been an adult authority figure for him, have I?"

"No, but that's what you're learning. And you're off to a good start."

Mrs. Jackson smiled at her older friend. "I was hoping that one tape you gave me had everything I needed to know," she said with a twinkle.

"Probably not," said Mrs. Peterson. "But if you want me to, I'll hang in there with you."

Julie Jackson reflected for a moment on her own parenting models, and on the choices that led her to the life she knew today. Mrs. Peterson was different. She wasn't big or strong. She wasn't flashy or pushy. There was a quiet resolve about her that Julie knew she needed for her son.

"What's next, Mrs. Peterson? I'm ready."

* * * * *

Mrs. Jackson spent the next few weeks learning to establish herself as the authority figure in the home, but without anger and threats. Once she knew Jimmy would go to recovery time when asked, she practiced getting control over food issues in the house. She cleaned up their diet, made mealtimes much more pleasant, and learned how to handle his whining for sweets.

The little things she practiced made such a difference.

"Jimmy, would you like peas or corn for a vegetable tonight?" she asked, giving him a little control in the right places.

"Would you like a bath or a shower tonight?"

"You know I don't like showers."

"Would you like me to read a story to you while you're taking your bath?"

"Yes, please," said Jimmy.

Sometimes he still screamed at her, and then she practiced some other new skills.

"I will not pick up my clothes. It's your job."

"Oh, Jimmy. It makes me sad when you scream, and I'm not exactly sure what to do about it. But don't worry, I'll get some ideas from my friends. We'll work it out."

Later she might say, "I'll be washing clothes that are put away in the hamper."

* * * * *

On Monday evenings, Mrs. Peterson kept emphasizing empathy.

"But sometimes I just want to yell and smack his face," said Julie Jackson.

"I know the feeling," said Mrs. Peterson. "And how do you think that would work?"

"Not so good. When I use anger and threats, he just resists harder."

"Still, it's hard not to use anger, threats, and lecture," empathized Mrs. Peterson.

* * * * *

Mrs. Peterson introduced the idea of chores to Julie Jackson.

"He's too young to be responsible for chores," Mrs. Jackson said aloud. I'll never get him to pay attention to chores, she thought silently. It's easier just to do the work myself.

"Some parents think it's just not worth the effort to get kids to do chores," said Mrs. Peterson. "But if you want Jimmy to keep making progress, it's got to be done."

Somehow, it wasn't as hard as she thought. Jimmy was starting to see his mom as being in charge around the house. He was going to recovery time when asked. He ate what was permitted. Bedtime wasn't an issue.

Jimmy chose taking out the garbage and sweeping the garage as his household jobs. Of course, he had to take care of his own toys and clothes, and clear the dishes after meals.

The night Jimmy forgot to push the big garbage container down to the street wasn't really his fault, Julie thought. They'd been out to the school concert, it was late, and Jimmy was tired. She hadn't reminded him. He was sleeping soundly as she looked lovingly at him curled up in bed. She started to leave the room and take the garbage out herself, but something stopped her. Gently she shook him.

"Jimmy. It's garbage night."

He opened his eyes and grabbed her hand. "Oh, mom. I'm tired."

She watched as he put a jacket over his pajamas, and his boots over his bare feet and pushed the big container to the street, and somehow she recognized the pride he had in himself for handling his job.

"It was so hard for me," she explained to Mrs. Peterson. "There's a part of me that just wants to protect him from any responsibility. I know it's not respectful of Jimmy, but I still feel it."

After some talk, Mrs. Peterson gave her Dr. Nolan's phone number. She'd worked with him before, and he had a way of helping parents get past the issues related to letting children become more independent. Sometimes parents unconsciously want to keep kids dependent so they'll feel needed by their children. Dr. Nolan dealt with such issues in just a few sessions, and Mrs. Peterson offered to use a special school fund to pay half the fee.

That same night they tackled the topic of TV and video games. By now, there was trust and affection between the two women, and they knew they enjoyed a strong respect for each another. But Julie Jackson looked anxious as Mrs. Peterson described how too much viewing affects young minds: TV was a companion for her.

"Five hours total per week?" she asked the school teacher for the second time.

"Of course, it's up to you, but that's what I'd recommend," replied Mrs. Peterson.

"What would we do without the TV on?"

"I've been eager to get to that question," said Mrs. Peterson. "Jimmy's behavior is getting so good at school, and now we're ready to help him develop the skills to make learning easy. Can I show you?"

This was the fun part for Mrs. Peterson. She showed Mrs. Jackson how Jimmy's difficulty with balance affected his seatwork and visual-motor skills. She shared the tricks of 22 years of teaching and learning. It was hard not to give her young friend too much all at once.

Less TV, lots of coloring, drawing, cutting, Legos, and balance activities on the balance board every day, she prescribed.

* * * * *

In January, Mrs. Peterson looked forward to their first meeting of the new year. Mrs. Jackson and Jimmy had traveled to Buffalo to visit with family during the holidays. Julie had been anxious about the trip: she often felt judged by her parents and sister. Jimmy had embarrassed her with his behavior in the past, and on their last visit there had been angry words.

On this Monday night, Mrs. Jackson dusted the snow off her hair as she entered the building and spoke briefly with the school custodian.

Mrs. Peterson was waiting, as usual, with coffee. They chatted about holiday things for a moment, then Julie Jackson started to cry, softly at first, then harder. In the quiet of the classroom, Mrs. Peterson wrapped her arms around Julie and held on tight.

After a few moments, Julie told her about their visit, and how scared she had been that she'd be judged harshly again. But for the first time since Jimmy had been an infant, the visit had gone well. Jimmy and his grandpa had even gone ice skating together, and once when Jimmy was getting a little wild playing with new toys, Julie had to ask him to go to recovery time for a few minutes, and to come back when he was calmer.

"I'll be back in a few minutes, Grandpa," he had said as he was leaving. "It won't take me long."

"There was a little incident on the playground today," said Mrs. Peterson. "Want to hear about it?"

"A problem?"

"No. Jimmy was playing with Josh and Jacob, as usual. And I was outside watching the children. I saw the boys running across the field, and Josh tripped and fell, and then came up yelling."

Mrs. Peterson went on. "He was just mad and embarrassed, so he was yelling at Jimmy and accusing Jimmy of tripping him when I walked up."

"Do you need a little help here?" I asked them. "Jimmy just smiled and laughed. 'He's just mad,' Jimmy said. 'Don't worry, we can handle it ourselves.'"

Mrs. Peterson drove home that night through the lightly falling snow. She knew that Jimmy and his mom were going to be all right. There was still some vision training to be done, and a few study skills to establish, and some careful reading practice to continue. But she knew.

Her husband met her at the door, and for a few minutes they talked before she excused herself. There was a letter she needed to write tonight.

She settled at her desk and thought about her oldest boy. He was somewhere in East Africa, part of a UNESCO medical team, and she missed him. He had managed to get a brief call through to her at Christmas, but it had been short. She began to write.

My Dear Jimmy,

I've met another little boy at school this year, and I've been wanting to tell you all about him. His name is also Jimmy. He's going to be fine, partly because of his strong mother, and partly because of all the things you helped me learn when you were his age . . . .

PREVENTING EARLY SCHOOL FAILURE

Bob Sornson

Sarah was in 3rd grade. She came slowly into the room, a bit shy about meeting this unfamiliar man wearing a suit and a tie. Sarah had been tested a lot recently, and most 3rd graders don't especially look forward to standardized testing.

I could see why her teachers loved her: there was a gentleness about her. The resource room teacher was with me, concerned that although Sarah did not qualify for any special services, she was struggling in academics and starting to be sad about school.

Not a terrible reader, Sarah could sound out most words, but it was slow. Spelling was not a strength—printing and writing were neat, but laborious. She spoke and listened well, and her balance was just shy of average. Visual-motor skills were underdeveloped, but coming along. Near-point vision seemed good, but depth perception was poor. Her visual-motor skills were about two years behind. Maybe the ear infections and antibiotics when she was two had slowed her down.

We laughed and skipped and balanced and read. She never stopped trying, not even when tasks were challenging. I guess that's when I started falling in love with her too.

Sarah's visual memory was underdeveloped, but I taught her to use it to remember a tough 3rd-grade spelling word: *catastrophe*. When we were done, she gave me a hug and ran back to class.

She didn't qualify for any extra help, but she was drifting behind. The curriculum train was moving down the track, and Sarah wasn't on board.

For some reason she wasn't quite as prepared for academics back in 1st grade as some youngsters. Her balance wasn't great. She didn't learn to ride a two-wheeler or skip until the summer after 1st grade. It took effort for her to use her hands and eyes close up, even as a 3rd grader. She was smart, as demonstrated by her listening and speaking skills, but she was unskilled at visualization or visual memory. She did her homework, even when it took a long time.

There are many kids like Sarah out there who are not quite ready for the demanding curriculum that they encounter in the early grades. Some have language or auditory processing delays, perhaps due to poor language models, too much video, ear infections, or allergies. Some have gross-motor coordination delays, perhaps due to lack of physical activity, poor balance, ear infections, lack of stimulation, or poor nutrition. Some kids just develop more slowly. Others have fine-motor or visual-motor delays, perhaps due to the lack of opportunity to play with crayons, paper, clay, paints, puzzles, blocks, and other manipulatives. Some children lack visual-motor experiences because they spend so much time with television and video games.

Still others have behavioral and social skill issues that make them unprepared for classroom instruction. Some are oppositional, lack persistence skills, or have not developed the ability to delay gratification. Some have just never had the opportunity to live with adults who are firm, loving authority figures. It takes a while for these kids to get the idea that they should listen to the teacher.

Without such basic skills, young students may not find success in the early grades—the grades that lay the foundation for their self-concept as learners. Kindergarten and 1st-grade teachers can pick them out. They know without any formal evaluations which students are struggling with language, listening, general motor development, hand-eye skills, or behavior skills. They know which students will struggle with beginning reading, remembering basic sight words, understanding number concepts, and trying to be good in school.

Sarah was luckier than many. Her supportive family was there for her, giving her messages of self-worth, ready to learn any new ideas that could help her. Sarah's teachers didn't care if she wasn't eligible for special services. A teacher assistant began to meet her before school every day and work on balance, depth perception, bilateral-motor skills, and visual-motor skills. Her classroom teacher adapted instruction so Sarah could work close to her instructional rate for much of the day. The special services teacher stayed after school three days a week to reteach basic number concepts and develop visual memory. Her parents supported all this at home.

* * * * *

In most American schools, we've tried so hard to intensify the curriculum that we've forgotten a few of these basic ideas:

• **Not all children are ready for instruction at the same level when they come to school.** In the typical 1st-grade classroom, children with normal intelligence will vary in developmental readiness by about four years. In a class of 6-year-olds, you will have some operating like 4-year-olds and others like 8-year-olds. This is normal variance. Expecting all young children to learn from the same materials at the same rate is not going to work.

• **All important basic skills should be learned completely until the concepts seem simple and easy to use.** Children should engage in pre-reading activities as long as necessary. Some countries delay formal reading instruction until 3rd grade. Children should read books that are easy. Most research indicates that books with 93–97 percent known words provide the best learning experience. Moving ahead in the curriculum before a child truly understands the basic ideas can create lifelong problems. How many children learn math facts (e.g., 7 + 4 = 11) without being able to quickly identify these numbers using manipulatives or understand how to use this math fact in the real world? Basic skills should be learned to mastery, then practiced (and played around with) to automaticity, so the children can use basic skills easily, without great concentration or effort. They should understand the concepts and skills so completely that they seem simple. This complete understanding should occur in the first few grades, no matter how much practice time is needed.

• **If we want a child to use a skill throughout life, it must be associated with joy.** Kids who learn to read joyfully will choose to read on their own. Kids who think mathematically with joy will balance their checkbooks as adults. Forcing children to practice tasks in the frustration range guarantees that they will avoid these tasks in the future. Safe classrooms in which every young child feels loved and respected are a basic requirement for good learning. Relationships with teachers and other students cannot be overlooked as they are essential to classroom performance.

Perhaps these ideas seem idealistic or impractical. I disagree. It is time to make a commitment that every young child will have a successful early learning experience. Anything else continues the system based on sort-and-select, allowing some capable children to drift behind while children fortunate enough to develop early readiness for academics succeed. Good jobs for poor learners no longer exist in this county. Lack of success in the first few grades is related to the likelihood of every risky adolescent and teen behavior, including substance abuse, violence, and early sexual activity. The cost to children who do not find success in the early grades is too great.

If only for the cost savings that will directly benefit school districts, it is time to reconsider early learning failure. By allowing children who have the potential for success to drift behind, many students will be eventually labeled as learning disabled or emotionally impaired. The added costs of these programs are substantial. In my district, we conservatively estimate the added cost per student receiving services from a classroom-based special program at $5,000 to $6,000 per year. This cost usually exceeds $50,000 over the student's school years. Many school districts identify 6 percent or more of students as learning disabled. But the research indicates that only 1 or 2 percent of students have true learning disabilities.

The programs and ideas described in this book represent some of the many ways to help nearly all children achieve learning success in the early grades. Success for All uses specific instructional techniques and support services to help children succeed. Instructional Support Teams create systems of support for both teachers and students, encourage collaboration, and improve instructional practices. Reading Recovery uses excellent instructional techniques for early readers. Soundfield FM amplification systems enhance the listening environment and improve attention and learning. Parents as Teachers demonstrates the effectiveness of helping parents learn how to help their children at home. All these approaches support the idea that nearly every child can get off to a good start in school.

Isn't it time to make the following new commitment to our children?

> In this school, we'll make sure that every child possible will learn the basic skills and concepts by the end of 3rd grade and experience joy and loving relationships in the process.
>
> Even though you come to us with different needs and experiences, we'll provide a rich, varied learning opportunity, and enough time to learn the important skills well.
>
> We'll pay close attention to your language skills, gross-motor skills, visual-motor skills, and social and behavioral skills. As soon as you are ready, we will help you develop basic reading, writing, listening, speaking, numeracy and reasoning skills.
>
> Whatever it takes, working with your parents, we will get the job done.

At this writing, Sarah is in 6th grade. I haven't seen her in a while. Recently, as I was leaving a school building, a burly, gruff-looking man approached me. "Aren't you Mr. Sornson?" he asked. Cautiously, I admitted that I was.

"I'm Sarah's father," he said. "You probably don't remember me. I just want you to know she's doing well. It took quite a while and a lot of work. We thought maybe she'd never really believe that she's smart." He grabbed my arm and went on. "It finally clicked. The learning began to come easier. She could spell and think in words better. She's doing well in 6th grade—all As and Bs. I thought you'd like to know. It means an awful lot to my family."

INDEX

References to figures are followed by the letter *f.*

ABOUT THE AUTHORS

Bob Sornson is a parent, author, administrator and presenter. He is the Executive Director of Special Education Services in Northville, Michigan, and the father of four children ranging in age from 5 to 15 years.

Known for his presentations to educators and parents, he is recognized for helping children, teachers, and parents learn to appreciate their unique gifts and abilities and to develop them to the fullest. He presents on topics including the prevention of early learning failure, motor and visual skill development, developing attention and behavior skills, and parenting.

Bob is the co-author of *Meeting the Challenge* (2000) along with Jim Fay and Foster W. Cline, M.D. In addition, he is the co-editor of *Teaching and Joy* (ASCD, 1997).

He can be reached at sornsoro@northville.k12.mi.us or at Northville Public Schools, 501 W. Main Street, Northville, MI 48167 (248-344-8443).

Richard L. Allington is the Irving and Rose Fien Professor of Elementary and Special Education at the University of Florida. Dick is a past President of the National Reading Conference. He was co-recipient of the Albert J. Harris Award from the International Reading Association for his work in reading and learning disabilities and has been named to the IRA Reading Hall of Fame. He has published over 100 research articles and several books, including *Classrooms That Work: They Can All Read and Write* and *Schools That Work: All Children Readers and Writers* (Longman), both co-authored with Pat Cunningham; *No Quick Fix: Rethinking Reading Programs in American Elementary Schools* (Teachers College Press) with Sean Walmsley; and *Teaching Struggling Readers* (IRA). His most recent book is *What Really Matters for Struggling Readers* (Longmans).

He can be reached at dickaufl@aol.com or at the University of Florida, 2403 Norman Hall, Gainesville, FL 32611 (352-392-9191).

Joyce McLeod is the author of *Math Advantage* (a kindergarten through grade 8 mathematics program) and *Harcourt Science* (a kindergarten through grade 6 science program). She was formerly Senior Vice President and Editor-in-Chief of Mathematics, Science, and Health for Harcourt School Publishers and now serves as Senior Editorial Consultant to the company. Joyce holds a visiting professorship in the College of Education and Human Development at Rollins College, Winter Park, Florida, teaching courses in mathematics content and methods for undergraduate education majors and teachers in the Master of Arts in Teaching program.

Joyce taught at the elementary school level and served as a trainer of teachers for many years. She holds a Bachelor of Arts degree in Elementary Education from the University of Central Florida, a Master of Education degree in administration and supervision, and a Specialist in Education degree in curriculum design from Rollins College. She is the recipient of the Outstanding Graduate in Teacher Education award given by Rollins College, the 1991 Natalie Delcamp Award for Excellence in Teaching at Rollins College, and the 1995 Alumni Association Professional Achievement Award from the University of Central Florida.

She can be reached at joycemcleod@harcourt.com or at ASCD, 1703 North Beauregard Street, Alexandria, VA 22311-1714 (800-933-2723).

Gary L. Hessler, Ph.D., has been involved in the field of special education since 1965, and he has been Consultant for the Learning Disabled with the Macomb Intermediate School District (Clinton Township, Michigan) since 1973. He has served as a special education teacher and teacher consultant, is nationally certified as a school psychologist, and is licensed as a psychologist in Michigan.

His major interests include the assessment and educational programming of individuals with specific learning disabilities. He has published in professional journals on the subjects of cognitive abilities and learning disabilities, and he is the author of the book *Use and Interpretation of the Woodcock-Johnson Psycho-Educational Battery* (Rev. ed., 1993).

He can be reached at Macomb ISD, 44001 Garfield Road, Clinton Township, MI 48038-1100 (810-228-3477).

Carol Flexer received her Ph.D. in Audiology from Kent State University in 1982. She has been at the University of Akron for 18 years, where she is a Professor of Audiology in the School of Speech-language Pathology and Audiology. Her special areas of expertise include pediatric and educational audiology. She has lectured internationally and authored more than 80 publications.

She co-edited the books *How the Student with Hearing Loss Can Succeed in College,* first and second editions, and *Sound-field FM Amplification: Theory and Practical Applications.* She authored the book *Facilitating Hearing and Listening in Young Children,* first and second editions, published in 1999.

Flexer is a past president of the Educational Audiology Association, a past Board member of Auditory-Verbal International, and a past president of the American Academy of Audiology.

She can be reached at The School of Speech-Language Pathology; Akron, OH 44325-3001 (330-972-8187).

James A. Tucker is a professor of educational psychology and the coordinator of the doctoral program in Leadership at Andrews University, Berrien Springs, Michigan. Jim served as director of the Pennsylvania Bureau of Special Education from 1993 through 1998 and helped implement the Instructional Support Team concept during those years. He has consulted with educational systems around the country and contributed to numerous publications.

He can be reached at Box 670, Niles, MI 49120 (616-471-3475).

Kenneth F. Pawlowski is currently the Principal of Silver Springs Elementary School in the Northville Public Schools, Northville, Michigan. He received his B.A. degree from Western Michigan University, his Master's and Specialist in Arts degrees from Eastern Michigan University, and his doctorate from Wayne State University. Pawlowski has served the Northville community for 30 years.

Silver Springs Elementary School is nestled within the Highland Lakes community. It is surrounded by residential homes, apartments, and condominiums. Students from a variety of cultural and socioeconomic backgrounds comprise the student body.

Pawlowski can be reached at pawlowske@northville.k12.mi.us or at Northville Public Schools, 501 W. Main Street, Northville, MI 48167 (248-344-8410).

Nancy Sornson is a special education teacher consultant in Brighton, Michigan. She currently works at Miller School, a kindergarten center where the prevention of early learning failure is a top priority. Through a careful assessment of language, motor, visual, and behavioral skills of young children, the staff works toward making sure each child has the tools needed to be successful in the early years of school.

Nancy has been a high school, middle school, and elementary educator, working with parents and teachers to maximize early learning skills and success.

She can be reached at nsornson@bas.k12.mi.us.

Edward E. Gickling, Ph.D., is best known for his pioneering work in curriculum-based assessment and is often referred to as "the father of CBA." He has been involved in various capacities with teacher training and staff development for more than 30 years. Gickling's teaching career has spanned four years in the public schools, six years as an assistant and associate professor of special education at the University of Tennessee-Knoxville, and nine years as an associate and full professor in special education at the University of Nevada-Reno. He served three years as Assistant Executive Director for Professional Development for the Council for Exceptional Children, and six years as an Instructional Assessment trainer for the Pennsylvania Instructional Support Team Project. He has consulted in 24 states and Canada and is currently in private practice contracting with school districts, intermediate units, and state departments of education. Gickling is often seen in the classroom demonstrating ways to work successfully with students who are at risk for academic failure. He has taught practitioners throughout the nation to use curriculum-based assessment to gather data on student learning and use the data to guide them in making appropriate curricular and instructional decisions that will lead to student success.

He can be reached at 5718 Pamela Drive, Centreville, VA 20120 (703-266-2545).

Verlinda P. Thompson, Ph.D., is currently the Associate Professor of Literacy Studies at Southern Utah University. In addition, she runs after-school reading programs for struggling readers with reading students at the university and with federal work-study students in America Reads. Previously, Thompson worked in public schools in New Mexico and Nevada, both in general education and in special education. For several years, she ran a private practice for struggling readers. In addition, Thompson has worked with reading research centers at both the University of Nevada-Reno and Southern Utah University.

Thompson received her Bachelor's and Master's degrees at the University of New Mexico in Albuquerque and her doctorate at the University of Nevada-Reno.

Robert E. Slavin is currently Co-director of the Center for Research on the Education of Students Placed at Risk at Johns Hopkins University and Chairman of the Success for All Foundation. He received his B.A. in Psychology from Reed College in 1972 and his Ph.D. in Social Relations in 1975 from Johns Hopkins University. Slavin has authored or co-authored more than 200 articles and 18 books, including *Educational Psychology: Theory into Practice* (Allyn and Bacon, 1986, 1988, 1991, 1994, 1997, 2000), *Effective Programs for Students at Risk* (Allyn and Bacon, 1989), *Cooperative Learning: Theory, Research, and Practice* (Allyn and Bacon, 1990, 1995), *Preventing Early School Failure* (Allyn and Bacon, 1994), *Every Child, Every School: Success for All* (Corwin, 1996), *Show Me the Evidence: Proven and Promising Programs for America's Schools* (Corwin, 1998), and *Effective Programs for Latino Students* (Erlbaum, 2000). He received the American Educational Research Association's Raymond B. Cattell Early Career award for programmatic research in 1986, the Palmer O. Johnson award for the best article in an AERA journal in 1988, the Charles A. Dana award in 1994, the James Bryant Conant Award from the Education Commission of the States in 1998, and the Outstanding Leadership in Education Award from the Horace Mann League in 1999.

He can be reached at Crespar-Johns Hopkins University, 200 W. Towsontown Blvd., Baltimore, MD 21204-5200 (410-616-2310).

Mildred M. Winter is Founding Director of the Parents as Teachers National Center, Inc. After serving as an early childhood teacher and administrator, Winter was appointed Missouri's first Director of Early Childhood Education. She helped develop the Parents as Teachers (PAT) program, initiated in 1981 to help parents effectively nurture their children's development and learning from before birth to age five, and was a key player in the enactment of Missouri's landmark Early Childhood Development Act of 1984. Winter has written numerous publications for professionals and parents on parent-child early education, and serves as consultant to state and national decision makers on early childhood family education and support programs and policy.

Winter was awarded the 1995 Charles A. Dana Foundation Award for Pioneering Achievement in Education for her work, which has become the springboard for linking neuroscience and early education. The resultant 1999 Born to Learn Curriculum and the accompanying video series translate information on early brain development into language parents can understand and apply, taking neuroscience from the laboratory into families' homes to enhance parenting and improve outcomes for young children.

She can be reached at Parents as Teachers National Center, 10176 Corporate Square Drive, Suite 230, St. Louis, MO 63132 (314-432-4330).

Lawrence J. Schweinhart is an early childhood program researcher and consultant. He has conducted research at the High/Scope Educational Research Foundation in Ypsilanti, Michigan, since 1975 and has chaired its research division since 1989.

Schweinhart is the lead researcher on the High/Scope Perry Preschool Study—the landmark study establishing the extraordinary human and financial potential of high quality early childhood programs; and the High/Scope Preschool Curriculum Comparison Study—which provides persuasive high-quality early childhood programs.

He received his Ph.D. in Education from Indiana University in 1975. Schweinhart has taught 4th and 7th grades as well as graduate and undergraduate college courses.

He can be reached at info@highscope.org or at High/Scope, 600 North River Street, Ypsilanti, MI 48198-2898 (734-485-2000).

Stephen Kay is the Principal of Scott Lane Elementary School in Santa Clara, California. This is his 10th year as a school principal. Stephen began his career in education as an elementary school teacher in 1968. Stephen left teaching in 1976 to pursue a career in the construction business. During the last five years of his tenure with the construction firm, he served as a school board member in San Jose.

Stephen Kay founded the 1,000 Days to Success program. This program guarantees that kindergarteners learn to read at 2nd-grade level by the end of their 2nd-grade year—or 1,000 days from when they were first enrolled. This high-profile program has caught the interest of schools across the country and has now been adopted by other schools. It has been incorporated, by Stephen Kay, Craig Wheaton, and Geoff Yantz, into a nonprofit corporation called the 1000 Days to Success School Network, Inc. (http://1000-days.org). Stephen and co-author Craig Wheaton have written about the experiences of their schools in the network in ASCD's *Educational Leadership* (October 1999) in an article entitled "Every Child Will Read—We Guarantee It!"

Kay can be reached at stevekay@aol.com or skay@scu.k12.ca.us, or at 5092 Durban Court, San Jose, CA 95138 (408-274-1909).

Craig Wheaton is an elementary principal at John C. Fremont School in Corcoran, California. In 1999 Craig was selected as one of four California administrators to serve as an intern at Xerox's Palo Alto Research Center (PARC). He spent 20 days at the research center during the summer of 1999 and currently serves as an intern in a joint program for the Association of California School Administrators and Xerox PARC. The purpose of the program is to help administrators understand the potential influences of technology on schools of the future, specifically in the year 2015. During the internship, 1999–2001, Craig presents to various corporate and educational groups on the implications of technology on education.

Wheaton can be reached at cwheaton@kings.k12.ca.us or at 500 W. Grove Street, Visalia, CA 93291 (559-992-5102).

Peter Kline has been teaching since 1958. In 1973, he co-founded the Thornton Friends School in Silver Spring, Maryland, and since 1985, he has been training teachers in schools, corporations, and public service organizations. Currently he is Chairman of the Board of Integra Learning Systems, a company that specializes in community building, teacher training, and curriculum or courseware development. He authored the Integra reading program, which has been used with great success in many different public school systems. He is the author of more than fifteen books, including *School Success, The Everyday Genius, Ten Steps to a Learning Organization,* and *Furnishing the House of Reason.*

Kline can be reached at peterkline@aol.com or at 19109 Johnson Road, South Bend, IN 46614 (219-291-1369).

Thomas R. Johnson, Ph.D., developed the theory and techniques of Project First Step in 1990/1991 while working on a Master's Degree specializing in Adapted Physical Education. Since then, the program has worked with more than 50,000 children and more than 5,000 teachers and staff in five states, the Peoples' Republic of China, and Canada. It has been funded by the state of Michigan, the W. K. Kellogg Foundation, and local grants and school districts.

Johnson and his wife, Cathy, train teachers and parents to use "snippets of time" to enhance the child's physical abilities so that he can succeed academically, socially, physically, behaviorally, and emotionally at his optimum level. Current brain research as well as practical and theoretical foundations form the basis for the theory.

Johnson is currently an Assistant Professor at Albion College in Michigan. He can be reached at Project First Step, Box 86, Gobles, MI 49055 (616-628-4321).

Jim Fay is one of America's most sought-after presenters in the area of parenting and school discipline. He has more than 30 years of experience as a teacher and school administrator, 15 years as a professional consultant and public speaker, and many years as a parent of three children. Jim's delightful sense of humor and storytelling style have made him a favorite personality on hundreds of radio and television talk shows.

Fay can be reached at School Consultant Services, 2207 Jackson Street, Golden, CO 80401 (800-424-3630).

Sally Ludwig holds degrees in English Language and Literature and in Community College Education. A faculty member with the William Glasser Institute, she provides training and staff development to educators around the nation. She lives in Guelph, Ontario, with her husband, Chris Mills.

She can be reached at 91 Foster Avenue, Guelph, Ontario, Canada N1H 3B5 (519-824-5979).

Kaye Mentley has worked as a teacher, director of gifted education, principal, and Assistant Superintendent for Instruction. She is a senior faculty member with the William Glasser Institute and has conducted training around the nation in Quality Schools, Leadership, Gifted Education, and Higher Level Thinking Skills. She is currently principal of the Grand Traverse Academy in Michigan.